There's Nothing That I Wouldn't Do If You Would Be My POSSLQ

Also by Charles Osgood:

*Nothing Could Be Finer
Than a Crisis That Is Minor
in the Morning*

There's Nothing That I Wouldn't Do If You Would Be My POSSLQ

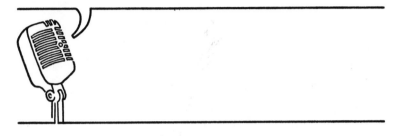

Charles Osgood

Holt, Rinehart and Winston
New York

Library of Congress Cataloging in Publication Data

Osgood, Charles.
There's Nothing That I Wouldn't Do If You Would Be My POSSLQ
I. Title.
PS3565.S53B7   811'.54   81-47460   AACR2
ISBN: 0-03-057667-9

First Edition

Designer: Amy Hill
Printed in the United States of America
10 9 8 7 6 5 4 3 2 1

Grateful acknowledgment is made for permission to
reprint lyrics from "Born to Run" by Bruce Springsteen
copyright © 1975 Bruce Springsteen & Laurel Canyon Music Ltd.
Used by permission.

To Jean, my POSSLQ

Contents

Nobody's Perfect

Special Days

People

The Government

Business

Obits

Light News Day

Love

Numbers

Preface

No two journalists approach a story in exactly the same way. But all journalists ask essentially the same question: What have we here? Some try to get to the bottom of a story by counting. In a war they count casualties. In a fire they count the number of alarms and firefighters and pieces of equipment. In all kinds of stories they try to price it out, getting to the reality of a thing by finding out how much it costs. This obsession with numbers reminds me of "The Count" on the television series "Sesame Street." I'm not sure that counting noses or dollars or any other quantifiable objects produces the objectivity a journalist desires or the insight into what-have-we-here that all of us look for. So I'm bad about numbers. That's one of my prejudices. Another is that officials of all kinds don't interest me much. I am much less interested in the effect the economy may have on a politician than I am in the effect the politician may have on people's lives, whether through the economy or anything else. Officials *are* people, but no more so than anyone else. Yet in the news business we are inclined sometimes to ignore a human event when it occurs, acknowledging its importance only when the hearings start, as if the hearings were the heart of it. The hearings are never the heart of it. So you will not find very many pieces about hearings in this book. Nor will you find very many officials and politicians, except in their role as human beings.

What we have here is human nature, glorious, hateful, funny, and sad. Those are the stories that make the best radio pieces, and those are the radio pieces I've picked out for this book.

You have to be bold, I have often been told,
Put suspense in each story—and shocks.
And it works without fail, as I've learned from the mail
That came in about vanishing socks.

Socks

The Great Sock Mystery

Have you ever wondered what happened to the socks that disappear in your washer? Or maybe it's your dryer that they disappear in. At any rate, they do disappear. This is not an occasional or isolated incident. Socks disappear all the time, and this has been going on now for years. Furthermore, an informal independent survey I've done on the subject indicates that sock disappearance is an almost universal experience. Everybody's socks disappear.

You would think, since sock disappearance is such a widespread and unexplained problem, that many Congressional committees and subcommittees would have studied the problem by now, investigated the mystery, held hearings, proposed legislation.

But they have not. So we must launch our own inquiry.

In a bureau drawer at home, I have maybe twenty socks. Not twenty pairs of socks, mind you, just twenty socks. All without mates. Each at one time belonged to a pair, but somewhere along the line, through a process not understood, the other socks disappeared. Now and again, a missing sock turns up under a bed or behind a bureau. But most socks, once they disappear, are never seen again.

Do washing machines eat socks? Washing machine manufacturers insist that they do not. Do dryers eat socks? Drying machine manufacturers (who turn out, incidentally, to be the same people) insist that they do not.

Where, then, are the socks? Is there some conspiracy afoot to take socks out of circulation for the benefit of the sock companies? Has anybody looked into whether the sock industry is making windfall profits because of the sock replacement necessitated by the sock disappearance?

One great problem is that there are no dependable statistics upon which one can base intelligent decisions on the subject. However, there are approximately 220 million Americans now, almost all of whom wear socks, two at a time. That's 440 million socks, just for openers. And most of us have several pairs of socks. Indeed, if each of us is missing as many socks as I personally am, the missing-sock figure is up into the billions. This is not small potatoes.

Among the questions I would like answered are these: Why is it that, of the twenty socks in a given bureau drawer, not one of them matches any of the others? Why is it that, even if you do find two of approximately the same color, one will come up to your ankle and the other darned sock will reach up to your knee? And speaking of darned socks, people used to darn socks. Nobody ever does any more. Why not? I would like to know.

Is there a nationwide sock-stealing ring, with agents who sneak into people's houses and pilfer socks out of washers, dryers, and hampers? And, if so, why do they never steal a whole pair, but only one sock at a time? And what is the market for the single socks they steal? What do they do with them anyway? Is there an underground supply of single socks, socked away somewhere? And finally, why this conspiracy of silence? Why has nobody blown the whistle on the great sock-disappearance scandal until now?

If you can unravel the mystery, let me know.

The New York Sock Exchange

Last week, right here, perhaps you heard,
We spoke of something quite absurd,
The fact that socks possess this trait:
They tend to deproliferate.
One sock, which makes up half a pair,
Will simply vanish in the air,
A universal mystery
Unparalleled in history.

And what is also unexplained
Is how this mystery remained
Unspoken of and, more's the pity,
Unprobed by any subcommittee.

In *Socks, Part One* one day last week,
In our constant, endless quest to seek
The answer to the great sock riddle
Of which we all are in the middle,
I asked if any of you know,
When men's socks vanish, where do they go?

The letters have been pouring in.
To read them all, I can't begin.
But of theories there is no lack.
I do think you are on the track.

Perhaps, as some of you suggest,
Martians take some, leave the rest.
For reasons out beyond the stars,
They need one sock of yours on Mars.
One Mary Gorman from St. Louis
Believes that maybe what is true is
Not that down the drain they're sucked,
But that certain socks just self-destruct.

Ruth Stearns of Rye says she believes
The fault lies with a ring of thieves.
Too mean to work, too proud to beg,
And all of whom have but one leg.
And that explains the quirk of fate
That leaves one sock without a mate.

Or here's a thought, perhaps debatable:
One sock is made biodegradable.

Many of your letters mention
Domestic grief, household dissension,
As husbands castigate their wives
When socks are missing from their lives.
We all have problems of our own.
It's nice to know you're not alone.

Many of you offered sock-washing tips,
Like joining each pair with some bands or some clips.
But the best idea, the greatest notion,
Came in from Queens. One H. Poloshjian
Suggests that maybe in his drawers
Are socks that might match some of yours.

He thinks there should be some device,
And possibly it would be nice
If matchups could be somehow made
Through systematic one-sock trade.
The time has come for such a change,
And hence, the New York Sock Exchange.

Words are important, you know that they are.
They can stand in your way, or can carry you far.

Words

The Elements of Guile

A week ago a new law went into effect in the State of New York requiring that all contracts and agreements up to $50,000 be written in common, everyday language, with words and phrases that have common, everyday meanings.

Now, the very idea that people should be able to actually understand the stuff they sign when they take out insurance policies, rent houses and apartments, borrow money, buy cars, and the like is a bit revolutionary. Most of us have always taken it for granted that it wouldn't do us much good to read the small print, since it is written by and intended for lawyers, who communicate in Latin and other ancient formulations incomprehensible to just plain, regular human beings.

Whereas, there came into being one week ago this day in the laws, regulations, and statutes of the State of New York a requirement that the writing in documents such as contracts and agreements covering transactions up to, but not more than, $50,000 be plain, everyday, ordinary English, such as the common man would understand.

And whereas, the legislature has chosen, decided, opted, and determined to thereby implicitly criticize, fault, and otherwise call into question the language now being used by the legal profession and the members thereof, suggesting that such modes of communication adversely affect the organization, administration, and efficiency of such transactions to the detriment of the consumer.

And whereas, such implicit criticism tends to foster the assumption that said modes of communication are in need of improvement, amelioration, betterment, and shaping up, I, Charles Osgood, being of passably sound mind and body and being duly signed, sealed, and delivered this seventh day of November 1978, do hereby state, say, suggest, and stipulate that such arbitrary and capricious harassment of lawyers and everything they stand for is based on a fundamental and basic misunderstanding of the role and function of the lawyer.

9

The role and function of the lawyer is not to simplify, clear up, speed, organize, and complete a given situation or circumstance. On the contrary, the role and function of the lawyer, properly understood, is to complicate, entangle, snarl, braid, and weave the elements of said circumstance or situation in such manner as to delay, slow up, prevent, discourage, and forestall the completion of same, or to cloud men's minds, the way Lamont Cranston used to.

The lawyer is specially trained in the art and science of transforming, changing, and metamorphosing even the simplest and most straightforward of notions into a maze from which there is no escape, into a haze resistant to all comprehension and understanding. Now, the ultimate expression of such expanded, prolonged, elongated, overdrawn prose is a document known (possibly for humorous reasons) as a brief.

To suggest, as the highly controversial new law in New York State does, that lawyers ought to, under certain circumstances, come right out and say what they mean is to strike at the very heart of the hallowed traditions of the legal profession. It's not only capricious and arbitrary, it's also a dirty trick.

Of course, lawmakers and legislators are also often lawyers themselves, which makes one wonder how this plain-talk law ever got through. I am told that there is considerable discussion now as to just what it means.

Sorry, No Spikka Da Hyperbole

In a court case in Fort Lauderdale, Florida, a judge has ruled that A. Douglas Henderson, the Avon cosmetics heir, has to pay his ex-live-in girlfriend, Pinky, only three percent of what she asked for in a so-called palimony suit. Ruled Judge Miette K. Burnstein, "The things lovers whisper in each other's ears do not necessarily hold up in a court of law. Hyperbole is the language of lovers."

Hyperbole is the language of lovers. Think of that! And Judge Burnstein went on to say in the Henderson case, "Such language alone cannot be said to form the basis of any contractual obligation. What pallor the courts would cast on courtship if they were to hold otherwise."

And so saying, the judge ruled that, instead of the nearly six million dollars demanded by the plaintiff from her ex-lover, $167,000 will have to do. Whatever the defendant might have promised in the heat of passion, the judge feels the plaintiff should have taken with a grain of salt.

"Adults have learned to view such language," says the ruling, "as being simply momentarily expressive of intense and immediate emotion and desire." Hyperbole is defined as extravagant exaggeration that depicts the impossible as actual, as in a "mile-high ice cream cone."

Well, we in the news business do not know any more than the next guy about ice cream cones, or about love, for that matter. But we do know a thing or two about politics. And it seems to me that what the judge has described is something that really rings a bell in an election year. I know what hyperbole is the language of. Hyperbole is the language of politics.

To illustrate my last remark,
I will not keep you in the dark.
To free the bee that's in my bonnet
I have composed a little sonnet:

If you will only cast your vote for me
And make of me the nation's chief of state,
You've no idea how absolutely great
And marvelous a President I'd be.

Iran would let our hostages go free,
The Russians right away would set a date
To pull their forces from the Afghan state,
And all the OPEC countries would agree
To set the price of oil nice and low,
And all the nations of the Middle East
(If you elect me President, I know)
Will stop their fighting at the very least.
Inflation and recession both will slow,
When all these stupid crises have been ceased.

Prosperity is what I guarantee—
And happiness, with no ifs, ands, or buts.
The tax bills that I bring would all be cuts
If you would only cast your vote for me.
I'd stimulate the nation's GNP.
I'd show you some intelligence and guts.
I'd be as straight as Mr. Nicklaus's putts.
Just put me into office, and you'll see
I'd run the government with common sense.
Believe me, I would do the job superbly.
The promises I make you are immense,
And yet, like lovers' vows, delivered verbally,
You must not hold me to them years hence.
I speak a language called Hyperbole.

Devaluation of the Word

Is it possibly true that those days are now dead
When we said what we meant and we meant what we said?
A buck was a dollar, a penny one cent,
And words had a value. We knew what they meant.

A word was like currency, backed up by gold
So a man could believe much of what he was told.
But it's only a dry, shifting desert of sand
If we don't know for what words or currency stand.

By the doings of countries or their central banks,
We've had devaluations of lira and francs.
The various monies all over the earth
Will fluctutate some as to what they are worth.
Depending on markets and factors of trade,
The relative levels of money are made.

But sometimes, for reasons of balance of payment,
Governments act in a sort of betrayment.
They still print this money the same as before,
But the money's not worth what it was any more.

And the reason they make this occasional move
Is the hope their economies then will improve.
And it works very often, though some people holler.
It worked when, last year, we devalued the dollar.

The economists' thinking proved out quite correct
And, on balance, produced the desired effect.
But there's also a currency used every day:
The words we employ in the things that we say.

Now, the word has a value that helps us relate
Whatever it is we are trying to state.

But it only had value if everyone knew—
If it meant the same thing both to me and to you.

There's a certain condition they used to call "war"
And that's what that word was supposed to be for.
Then all the fighting and shooting would cease,
And you'd have something else—which we used to call
    "peace."

But now the words have to be carefully studied,
For somehow the meanings got terribly muddied.
And unless you appreciate how they are used,
It is possible one could get rather confused.

For how could you know what it was that you heard
The day they devalued the word?

Some men do it on purpose, distort what they say.
And sometimes it's simply a verbal decay.
But we woke up one day from our afternoon nap
And discovered this great credibility gap.

And out of what once were reliable sources
We now were confronted by sinister forces
And code words were used with subliminal meaning
To people with this or that kind of a leaning.

When language devalues, it's all connotation
And people are skeptical throughout the nation.
They hear all these statements on gasoline prices,
The reasons for why there's an energy crisis.
And still there's doubt. Or now we've come to feel
They're passing out words but that words aren't real.

They're no longer operative. Words, we are told,
Are no longer backed by reality's gold.
We check out words in our books and divertissements,
Movies and newspapers, broadcast advertisements.

Words get devalued so something will sell.
Watch that old pea, now. It's under that shell.
Some of the words are the same as before,
But they just aren't worth what they were any more.

Wheelbarrows of words—only partly believed,
Because so many times we were badly deceived.
The world of ideas became sadly absurd
The day they devalued the word.

A Minor Ms. Understanding

The subject of this morning's rhymes
Is that great, gray lady, *The London Times*.
The Times of London, great and gray,
Is the arbiter, some people say,
Of the English language, that it might teach
The proper use of the parts of speech.
To protect the Queen's English from verbal crimes
Is seen as the duty of *The London Times*.

As to word and phrase, as to style and form,
The Times establishes the norm.
But respected as its judgments are,
This time it may have gone too far.
For the latest dictum of the paper is
That there's no such title as the title Ms.
Now, what a controversial matter this is,
That a woman must be either Miss or Mrs.

As rich in tradition as the Big Ben chimes
Are the stately columns of *The London Times*.
And now *The Times*' impact has been put on trial
In a supplement to its book of style.
From this point on, *The Times* directive is,
There'll be no more using of the title Ms.

From *The Times* news column Ms. has simply vanished.
It's been excommunicated, banned, and banished.
There are valid reasons, we are told,
For driving Ms. out into the cold.
Trevor Fishlock of the paper's staff
Dismisses Ms. in a paragraph.
A forlorn and fatherless little word,
Motherless too—why, it's just absurd.
Artificial, ugly, silly, doesn't mean a thing.

And here's the part that must really sting:
It is rotten English, says Fishlock there.
Ms. should be junked, should be allowed no air.

The idea of Ms. was that the title carried
No information as to who was married.
There's no marital status in the title Mr.,
And it seemed to many a feminist sister
That a woman shouldn't have to go through life
Addressed as either single or somebody's wife,
A married Mrs. or a single Miss.
Now what they decided to do about this
Was to make up a title neither fish nor fowl.
Just an M-S-period, without a vowel.

The same abbreviation, somebody quipped,
Was already used for "manuscript."
And MS had other meanings, if you please,
Such as multiple sclerosis, a well-known disease.
But Ms. caught on, as we all have seen.
It became the name of a magazine.
And some dictionaries jumped on the fad.
The Times of London thinks that's too bad.
Funk & Wagnalls has a definition of its own:
"Title of a woman, marital status unknown."
But the lexicographer apparently forgot
That the woman surely knows if she's married or not.
And furthermore, *The Times* insists, Ms. fails to do
That which it presumably intended to.
If it meant to leave the status out, it doesn't do it.
All Ms. does is call still more attention to it.

But one newspaper will avoid such crimes,
For Ms. is now Ms.-ing from *The London Times*.
In time, it's a judgment that we all can make:
If *The Times* of London made a big Ms.-take.

What God Hath Wrought in the Past, He Don't Wring That Way No More

This being the first Monday in September, today is Labor Day. This is one holiday they didn't have to horse around with and move to a Monday, because it was already on a Monday. This is the day that the workingman is supposed to take off so that he can look back with satisfaction on the fruits of his labors over the last year—to point with pride to what he has wrought.

Speaking of the word "wrought," what is the present tense of the verb of which "wrought" is the past participle? We refer often (we just did refer, in fact) to what people have wrought, or what God hath wrought. But how does one express what is *being* wrought? Or what is *about to have been* wrought?

Robert Benchley raised the question one time, without really answering it: What is the present tense of the verb which, in the past perfect, is "have wrought" or "has wrought" or "had wrought"? In fact, even simple past doesn't seem to work with "wrought." Just doesn't sound right to say, "Here is something I wrought yesterday." But what ought to be the simplest form of all—the present—seems not to exist.

I asked around here this morning and got a couple of different answers. One of my esteemed colleagues was pretty sure that "wrought" is the past participle of the verb "to wreak." I wreak, you wreak, he, she, or it wreaks. As in wreaking havoc. As far as I know, havoc is about the only thing people ever really do wreak and, in that case, it would hardly be the constructive sort of thing that you'd be likely to do on Labor Day— to look back on the havoc you have wrought. Maybe there are a few things that one can wreak besides havoc. (Oh, yes! Hurricanes wreak devastation sometimes.)

Now, the dictionary seems to bear me out on this. According to our fat Webster's, "wreak" (with a "w") is from the Middle English "wreken," which meant to drive out, to punish, or to revenge, and seems to have the word "wreke" in it. Whereas "wrought" is in there only as an adjective or a past participle.

No clue at all as to what it's the past participle of, however, except to say it is from the Middle English "worken" (which would seem to have more to do with work and labor and Labor Day). It was also an Old English word "Geworht"—which is also cited as a semantic source—and it is from that that we get the word "wrought" as in "wrought iron" or a "finely wrought drawing."

However, this still leaves quite unsatisfied the need for a present tense for "wrought." And another one of my colleagues here is of the opinion that if you want to have wrought something, then what you need to do is to go out and "wring" whatever it is you wish to have wrought. Says he, that which has been wrung is wrought. So, back to the dictionary.

To wring is from the Middle English "wringen," which meant to compress by twisting or squeezing, as in, "I think I'm going to wring your neck." So that seems out for our present purposes.

And here you are on Labor Day, 1976, and you're trying to look back on what you have "wrung" or "wreked" or "wrought" in the past year, and here we are giving you something vexing like this to boggle your poor, weary head. "Vex" (of course) from the Middle English "vexen," meaning to trouble or to distress.

Well, at any rate, it is Labor Day today, and just possibly it will give you some amusement on this day off, something to run through your head, to contemplate what things you might "wring" or "wreak" or "wreke" in the year to come.

Unless, of course, you already know the present tense of "wrought" . . . in which case, what is it?

If you enjoy the work you do,
Then you are one of the lucky few.

Work

How Come Nobody Can Do Anything Right Any More?

There is an epidemic of incompetence. It used to be that every so often you'd run into somebody who wasn't very good at what he did. Nowadays it seems nobody is able to do anything right. Have you noticed that? Governmentally, militarily, politically, commercially, financially, managerially, secretarily, you name it. Nobody can do it any more.

We make things so poorly they break, and when they break nobody can fix them. We have writers who can't write, actors who can't act, painters who can't paint. We have teachers who can't teach and schools where the students don't learn anything. We have leaders who don't lead, profit-making corporations that lose money, and in the Major League All Star game last night, we had an All Star second baseman who couldn't field a ground ball and an All Star pitcher who threw two wild pitches. And before the game, while a singer who couldn't sing sang the national anthem, there was an all-star fireworks display and the rockets landed in the hills behind Dodger Stadium's centerfield wall and started a huge brush fire.

There are certain professions in which incompetence is not tolerated for long. Brain surgery comes to mind, for example. Another area of endeavor where a high price must be paid for not being any good at it is armed robbery. Armed robbery is a risky enterprise at best, and does not usually attract your intellectual types. But there are certain minimal standards of competence required in the armed-robbery business, failing which the individual perpetrator is likely to find himself behind bars. Provided, of course, that some incompetent cop, prosecutor, judge, or jailer does not intervene.

In Stockton, California, yesterday, Allen Roth allegedly handed a bank teller a note saying, "I have a gun. Give me three thousand dollars or I'll kill you." The teller gave him the money and pushed a silent-alarm button. Roth then did a very foolish thing. Instead of getting out of there and disappearing as fast as he could, he telephoned for a taxicab and waited for the cab in the bank lobby. The police got there before the cab did, and now Roth is in all sorts of trouble. He should never have robbed the bank, of course, but if he was going to rob the bank he should never have tried to make his escape by calling for a cab. Taxicab companies are notoriously incompetent.

In Los Angeles, meanwhile, a masked armed robber took $180 from a shop cash register, and then his incompetence began to tell. He put the money in a bag and the bag broke and the money fell all over the place and while he was bending over to pick up the money his shotgun fell apart and he left the butt behind and as he ran away his mask slipped off and people got a good look at him. Then, an hour and a half later, he and his driver came back to the place, for what reason we don't know. Maybe to find the missing piece of shotgun. Anyway, it was a mistake. He was recognized and police found and fitted the shotgun butt to the barrel they found in the car.

Just between you and me, I'm glad that I'm not a brain surgeon or an armed robber. Fortunately, in the news business, competence is not considered absolutely necessary.

I'd Rather Be a Side-Splitter than a Set-Up Man

Already a best-seller among the various publications of the U.S. Government Printing Office is a new book called DOT. That's an acronym for *Dictionary of Occupational Titles.* It's a handy little reference work that took fifteen years to compile and can be found in all U.S. state employment security offices and in many schools, libraries, and corporate personnel officers.

Thumbing through DOT, you can find many jobs with absolutely fascinating titles. Can you imagine what a bottom-duster is? Or a back-washer? Well, a back-washer is somebody who tends machines in a textile plant, and a bottom-duster turns out to be a dust-brusher in a shoe factory. DOT also advises us that a side-splitter is not a joke or a comedian, but a fellow who works in a meat-processing plant. There are ribbers who work in meat-processing plants, too. The ribbers presumably don't rib their co-workers all that much—they confine their ribbing to the meat. Although it must be tempting to rib the side-splitters a little bit or pick on the pickle-pumpers, another category in the same business listed in the DOT book.

A gondola girl, whose title suggests the canals of Venice, needs no boat to do what she does, no oar nor mandolin. Gondola girls replenish the shelves in supermarkets.

Bed-setters and sheet-turners have nothing to do with either beds or sheets. A bed-setter is a stoneworker and a sheet-turner works in the veneer-and-plywood industry.

DOT says a crib operator serves food in industrial plants. On the other hand, a meal man doesn't have anything to do with meals. He works in a grain or feed mill.

A kiss-setter can be a man or a woman in a candy plant. A fellow who operates engines to move logs in a logging camp is known as a donkey-puncher, and a banana messenger is somebody who helps care for perishable fruit.

If you should apply for a job as a set-up man, that may be all right, but you'll have to define what it is you set up. The

DOT lists different kinds of set-up men. Some of them set up machinery and others set up dentures.

Now, where do you suppose you'd go to look for a de-hairer? Well, at first blush you might say a barbershop, but you'd be wrong. A de-hairer is somebody who works in the glue-and-leather-making business. And a dye barber is not a barber either. He works in a machine shop as a rough finisher.

An air-filler, despite what some people may say, is not somebody who does what I do on the radio. An air-filler is an inspector in a barrelmaking plant.

A scalper, at least according to this *Dictionary of Occupational Titles*, has nothing to do with the selling of Super Bowl tickets. A scalper is somebody who works in mining or quarrying.

An agitator means to cause no political trouble. DOT says an agitator works in chemicals. Well, come to think of it . . .

A knockdown man is not Larry Holmes or someone in his profession. Knockdown men are incinerator-plant attendants.

Almond-knockers are harvest hands, not people who go around saying, "Boy, are these terrible almonds!"

A necker makes jewelry cases.

Should you be visited by a rub-out man one of these days, do not get down on your knees and plead for your life. A rub-out man is nothing more than somebody who prepares paint samples.

Hanging In There

If at first you don't succeed, the saying says that then
The thing to do is not give up but try, try again.
But if at first you don't succeed,
A saying isn't what you need.
What you need are some reasons why
It might be worth your while to try.
And now, my friends, would you believe,
I've got a few right up my sleeve.

You say you didn't get the job? You didn't make the sale?
Your book has been rejected, and it's thumbs-down now, you
    fail?
Well, before you throw the towel in, before you call it quits,
Consider these examples while you're down there in the pits:

Lust for Life by Irving Stone, the story of Van Gogh,
Was turned down by many publishers—seventeen said no.
The public wouldn't buy this book, Irving Stone was told.
At last report now, twenty-five million copies have been sold.
And Vincent knew the bitter sting of mean rejection's knife.
Of paintings, he sold only one—one painting all his life.
And Julia Child's first cookbook, she would be the first to say,
Was rejected, failed as flat-out as a novice's soufflé.

Dr. Seuss, the brilliant writer that the kiddies just adore,
Has lots of his rejection slips. Well, maybe twenty-four.
"The Muppet Show" is popular, with its funny, clever scenes.
But for twenty years the network couldn't see the show for
    beans.
Beethoven's "Fidelio" was a miserable flop.
It was after the composer died that it came out on top.
And the emperor for whom Wolfgang Amadeus Mozart
    wrote
Criticized one of his operas; said it had too many notes.

Many great composers who are honored so today—
Berlioz and Franck and Shostakovich and Bizet—
Had to cope with great rejection, had to do the best they
    could,
Even though some critics said their music simply wasn't any
    good.
The Beatles were rejected, and it seemed they might be
    through,
Before Parlaphone took them on in 1962.
"A balding, skinny actor"—it's in black and white right
    there—
"Can dance little," says the sheet, rejecting Fred Astaire.
The Steelers once rejected a young quarterback (the dolts)
So they later had to face him—John Unitas of the Colts.

The inventor, Robert Fulton, had a quite inventive dream
Of ships that would be powered not by wind, you see, but
    steam.
"Fulton's Folly," they all called it, it would never leave the
    dock.
And the man who was behind it was, of course, a
    laughingstock.
Chester Carlson went to Kodak; "no, no, no," he heard them
    say
To the process that's referred to as xerography today.
And a young, part-time reporter in 1933,
Who worked for just a buck a day at the old KTUT,
Was told he'd better stick to print, air talent wasn't his.
"Sorry, Walter," he was told, "but that's the way it is."

To fail is not the terrible disaster it may seem,
If you just hang in there long enough and hold on to your
    dream.
To dream, as William Shakespeare wrote, "To dream, ah,
    there's the rub."
And if at first you don't succeed, well, welcome to the club.

28

Sixty Reasons Your Idea Is No Good

If you have an idea about how to solve some problem, you are in for a disappointment. No matter how wonderful your idea is (and no matter how terrible the problem is that your wonderful idea solves), when you take the idea to the person or department you think could do something about it, they will tell you they can't do it and to forget it. The Corporate Relations Department of the Southland Insurance Company has worked up a little list of sixty ready-made reasons why a given idea won't work. And my idea was to reword the list into a little poem.

Your idea would work, you are sure that it would—
But they shake their heads slowly and say it's no good.
"We've tried that before," is the first on the list
Of reasons why ideas are quickly dismissed.

"Our place is different," is grouse number two.
Three is: "It costs too much money to do.
And even if we had financial ability
It isn't our (number four) responsibility."

"Take it to Harry, to George, or to Bob.
I'd try it, of course, but it isn't my job."
That's excuse number five for somebody to say
"Please take your proposal and just go away."

Number six: "We're too busy." Seven: "Too strange;
Your idea is a too radical sort of a change."
"We don't have enough research, enough time or men,"
Are the reasons we're numbering eight, nine, and ten.

"It would make our equipment become obsolete."
"Our office is too small; we'd need a whole suite."
"If it weren't impractical, then I would try it . . .
But I'm sure that the staff here would just never buy it."

"Your timing is wrong and we can't do it now."
"Company policy will not allow . . . "
"It would run up our overhead too, furthermore . . . "
"And we've never done anything that way before."
Ideas aren't welcome, as well you have seen,
For those reasons: eleven through number eighteen.

"It is too ivory-tower. It's pie in the sky.
I don't like your idea, and I'm telling you why.
We don't have the authority, don't have the clout—"
Two more of the reasons your idea is out.

"You're right in your feeling. We should make a move,
But let's do something else. No, they'll never approve."
"The planning committee will want other names."
"Your proposal is sure to be shot down in flames."

"I don't see the connection. Let's shelve it for now."
"I'd do it, but really, I just can't see how."
"Has anyone tried that? There must be some reason."
"It's the wrong time and place, the wrong day, the wrong
    season."

"I know someone who tried that one time in one place,
And what did he do? He fell flat on his face."
Reasons thirty through thirty-nine all seem to state
That you're too young or old or too early or late.

"It just might have worked if we'd tried that before,
But we're well past that point. It won't work any more.
We should study it further. It cannot be done,"
Is reasoning forty up through fifty-one.

"We would, but you can't teach an old dog new tricks"
Is excuse numbers fifty-three, -four, -five, and -six.
"It would be too upsetting and far too much trouble.
It would cause our expenses and taxes to double."

"Your idea is clever, it does sound like fun,
But around here that isn't the way things are done."
Excuse number sixty, I am sorry to say,
Is: "We always or never have done it that way."

So, if some inspiration should hit you, well, let it,
And here's what to do with your brainstorm: Forget it!

The Difference Between You and Me

You are just wasting your time there
As you sit very still in your chair.
It is not the same thing as when I'm there
Contemplating some problem or care.

You must be terribly lazy
Just as shiftless and slow as can be.
But it would be incredibly crazy
To attribute the same faults to me.

You are just idly dreaming
Concocting some pie in the sky.
You are not as constructively scheming
Or as wonderfully clever as I.

When you err you're a terrible bumbler—
A goof-off without any style.
But mistakes do not make me the humbler,
"I suppose we're all human," I smile.

When it's you who backs out of a fight, dear,
It is such a disgraceful defeat,
Whereas if I should pull out of sight, dear,
It is then called "strategic retreat."

When it's you reading some periodical
Sitting back on some comfortable perch
It's a waste, whereas I'm so methodical
That it goes by the name of research.

When I spend, it's my generous way, dear,
And my kind disposition, so sunny.
But when you do, you know what they say, dear,
Soon occurs to a fool and his money.

When I wisely refuse to be spending,
It is only the shrewd thing to do.
I am not being cheap or intending
To be an old tightwad like you.

We both like to eat, you and me, though,
From a groaning board, ample and big,
It's not quite the same, don't you see, though.
I'm a gourmet. You're a pig.

And the same thing applies to our drinking.
To the wine store both you and I rush.
But we're basically different, I'm thinking.
I'm a wine connoisseur. You're a lush.

You may think I'm a plain politician
With my eye on political booty.
But I'm really devoid of ambition
What I'm doing is doing my duty.

You are nosy and I am observant.
The events of the day have me shook.
I'm a wonderful national servant.
While you, I suspect, are a crook.

In affairs of mankind and of nations
And the various acts that they do,
There can be different interpretations
Depending on just who is who.

You accuse me of just doing nothing.
It's not true, as a matter of fact.
I am far, far beyond doing nothing—
I am boldly refusing to act.

Having What It Takes

Let's say that you are the chief of police somewhere, charged with the responsibility of finding and hiring good people for your police force. The first question you ask yourself is, What makes a good cop? The answer involves some considerations you may not have thought of: height, teeth, vision, and ability to climb over a wall, for example. You may have to take some of those things into consideration whether you want to or not.

Okay, chief, one thing you will, of course, have to keep in mind when trying to hire people for your police force is that the federal government is going to be all over your back if you fail to hire enough women and minority members. The Law Enforcement Assistance Administration has been known to cut off all federal grant money to law enforcement agencies that fail to implement so-called affirmative-action programs. However, as you try to dance around that pitfall, you may find yourself falling into some other pit because the rules and regulations as to who qualifies to be a policeman vary widely from place to place. The Urban League explored that very thing in a workshop project in New York City yesterday.

In Arlington County, Virginia, the rule is that police officers must be at least five feet eight inches tall. Now, it just so happens that ninety-four percent of all women are under five feet eight inches tall, and are therefore disqualified as police officers before they even get the application form filled out. But why should a police officer be five feet eight? Once upon a time, New York City used to work on the theory that since police sometimes direct traffic, they would have to see over the tops of cars. But you know as well as I do that in a given traffic jam there are usually one or two buses and some tractor trailers, and the police officer would have to be about twenty feet tall to see over the tops of those. New York City, incidentally, is now hiring shorter men and women, and they do just about as good a job as taller officers when it comes to untangling traffic jams. Which is to say not much good at all.

One police department studied by the Urban League project required each police officer to have six molars on at least one side of the mouth. That would mean that anybody without wisdom teeth is out. It may be a little hard to see what value wisdom teeth might have in enforcing the law, since wisdom teeth have nothing whatever to do with wisdom. Apparently that rule originated back when police had to bite off the ends of linen pouches of powder for muzzle-loading rifles—something that hardly ever comes up any more.

In Jersey City, New Jersey, to be a police officer you have to be able, among other things, to scale an eight-foot wall. Lee Reynolds, who is the Urban League project director, says, "We drove all over Jersey City and could not find a single eight-foot wall." This suggests that the actual necessity of climbing eight-foot walls while on patrol in Jersey City is minimal. But the requirement is still there.

Women may find that one hard to meet. And some may have difficulty in dragging a one-hundred-fifty-pound dummy (which is another requirement in some departments). Again, though Lord knows police officers do have to deal with some dummies in the course of their work, it is not often necessary to drag them. No matter how much they weigh.

The federal government would like to see some of the departments change the rules so that women and minorities could meet them more easily. Some departments reject applicants with poor credit ratings. Reynolds says with women and minorities you're going to find poor credit ratings because of the low-paying jobs they've been able to get in the past, and because women traditionally get bad credit ratings just because they're women.

So, in your job as police chief, you may find yourself in a squeeze play with Washington on one side and an eight-foot wall on the other. Perhaps you can get the rules changed. But that's not always easy. All those one-hundred-fifty-pound dummies, you know.

If best-laid plans of mice and men
Worked out all right now and again
I think that would be very nice.
Nice for the men, nice for the mice.
Unfortunately, they do not.
They gang aglee an awful lot.

Nobody's Perfect

Merry Comsat to All and to All a Good Grief

'Twas two weeks before Christmas and down at the Cape,
The Satcom III satellite seemed in great shape.
They had launched it last Thursday. They did so at night.
And the witnesses called it a beautiful sight.

A picture-book launch, as it rose in the air,
And the tracking confirmed it was just about where
They had hoped it would be, right according to plan,
So says NASA's Jim Lacey, and RCA's man,

John Williamson, says it looked good to him, too.
Satcom did what its planners had planned it would do.
It went into an orbit and looped 'round the earth.
It was tracked at Earth stations, from Beltsville to Perth.

But something has happened, it pains us to tell,
For the flight of the Satcom did not come out well.
It's a very nice satellite, nice as can be,
The one that is missing, the late Satcom III.

It was shaped like a box, about five feet by four,
And it weighed just a ton, maybe just a bit more.
It had twenty-four channels, which made it a peach,
For the channels were leased at a million bucks each.

RCA had the customers all set to go,
And had already laid out a whole lot of dough.
Twenty million to build it, and that's just for starts,
Electronic components and satellite parts,

And thirty more million for boosting and such.
To launch such a vehicle costs pretty much.
And they bought some insurance. Five million they paid
(Which may be the brightest decision they made).

For today there are people quite red in the face.
Satcom III is now missing. It's lost out in space.
After staying in orbit, this craft, Satcom III,
Was to seek out a spot where they thought it should be,

Which was synchronous orbit in station specific,
Twenty-two thousand miles high above mid-Pacific.
As wild leaves that before the wild hurricane fly
When they meet with an obstacle mount to the sky,

So satellite engines are duly inspired
Whenever their kick motors come to be fired,
Which was done from New Jersey, the spokesmen now say,
By Americom, wholly owned by RCA.

They said not a word, but went straight to their work,
And pushed the right button, then turned with a jerk,
For the tracking display that the Satcom was on
Showed a very strange thing: the Satcom was gone.

In a twinkling Americom got on the phone
With satellite stations it happens to own.
They said, "Please let us know if you happen to see
A runaway object, because Satcom III

Has vanished, it seems, away somewhere in space,
And we can't seem to find it around anyplace."
They called NASA and NORAD and Telesat, too,
Western Union and COMSAT, and asked them to do

Whatever they could to explain where it went,
This object on which so much money was spent.
On NORAD, on COMSAT, on NASA, and all,
From the top of the porch to the top of the wall,

Look under the bed or in back of the moon.
We hope you can find it and find it quite soon.

It is quite disconcerting, the experts all say,
To have it just suddenly vanish this way.

But an RCA man, with his dimples so merry,
Is glad about one thing. Glad? Oh, yes. Very.
And I heard him exclaim to his team, as he hollers:

"We have an insurance policy for Satcom III which, if it
fails during launch, in the first ninety days, will pay
us seventy million dollars."

Anybody Got Any Suggestions About What I Should Do with All These Brooms?

In a room somewhere in Kansas City at this very moment, there are over two thousand brooms tucked away. Brooms that nobody knows quite what to do with. Here's what happened.

A group called the Congressional Reform Committee (which wants to elect enough Republicans to Congress to make Republican John Rhodes the Speaker of the House, rather than Democrat Thomas P. O'Neill) got to thinking that they needed a symbol, something to use at the Republican Convention that would stand for what they wanted to do: sweep clean. And what could possibly be better for that than a broom? So they went out and bought enough brooms so that most of the 2,259 delegates at the convention would be able to have one.

The committee paid a dollar apiece. They were, after all, new brooms—new brooms to sweep clean, you see? And the plan was that when Congressman Rhodes would be introduced to the convention as its permanent chairman, the delegates would get up and wave the brooms and hold them up in the air so that the folks in the television audience could see them and get the message.

Well, it seemed like a pretty good idea, and very dramatic, too. But there were two people that the committee had not figured on. One was the Kansas City fire marshal. He was not at all pleased with the broom idea, because the aisles there in the convention hall are very narrow—so narrow that the brooms would be as wide as the aisles. So, if there were a fire and people were trying to get out of there, there would be brooms all over the place to trip on and get in the way. Besides, the straw itself could catch fire, turning the brooms into torches. No, the fire marshal was not at all enthusiastic about the broom idea. Except in a negative way. He enthusiastically did not want those two thousand brooms in there.

The other person who did not like the broom idea very much was Ody Fish. He is the manager of the convention for the party. And, to him, the picture of two thousand people waving brooms did not seem quite to convey the image that the Republican Party was striving to create at the convention. So he vetoed the idea.

There were many meetings on the subject. Steve Bell, a Senatorial aide who works with the committee, says, "Lord, we were spending all our time worrying about brooms!" He says, "I bet we had ten meetings—here and in Washington—about the brooms."

At the moment, the way things stand, when Congressman Rhodes is introduced as permanent chairman, the Clean Sweep Campaign will be launched with pictures of brooms.

Now, if the idea is for the two thousand brooms to be replaced with two thousand pictures of brooms, that must mean that somewhere there are two thousand pictures of brooms being printed. Whoever is doing the job must wonder why anybody would want two thousand copies of a picture of a broom.

If the committee gets Ody Fish and the fire marshal to change their minds and allow the use of real brooms, then the two thousand pictures of brooms will be useless. Unless, of course, they think of some way to use both the brooms and the pictures of the brooms.

It seemed like a good idea at first,
But the new broom bubble now has burst.
To use the brooms was not the wish
Of the fire marshal or Ody Fish.

To greet Convention Chairman Rhodes
A lot of brooms were bought—yes, loads.
But it seemed to Fish that such broom-waving
Was not a good way of behaving.
(Besides, there was the plaintive beef
Of Kansas City's fire chief.)

And so, the way things stand today,
The broom idea is swept away.

And pictures of brooms will be used instead—
Or so a committee spokesman said.

Have you ever tried to sweep a room
With a picture of a broom?
Well, if you have something you need to sweep,
You know where you can find brooms—cheap.

Please Do Not Feed the Paper Tiger

Here's a real governmental breakthrough: After sixty years, the federal government has now decided to do away with the odd-ball eight-by-ten-and-a-half-inch size of its official stationery and to go with the same size stationery practically everybody else uses (which is eight and a half by eleven). Uncle Sam has been raring back to make this stupendous change for quite a while now, with committees and commissions and working groups and advisory panels and what-all, holding meetings, collecting data, making recommendations, and all that stuff, until now, finally, a firm decision has been made. This is one thing the government can do something about.

Effective January first, bureaucrats are ordered to use only as much eight-by-ten-and-a-half-inch stationery as they then have on hand, and after that stock is used up, to send out whatever it is they're sending out on regular eight-and-a-half-by-eleven-inch paper.

The federal government (please do not laugh)
Uses paper eight inches by ten and a half.
While industry most everywhere under heaven
Uses paper that's eight and a half by eleven.
The difference would seem to be inconsequential,
But in the bureaucracy, it is essential
To do everything in a uniform way.
To follow the rules and whatever they say.

And the rules about paper, those policy laws,
Were set down in the twenties by someone named Dawes
Who headed a printing advisory group
That chased down the data, the paperwork poop,
And decided there had to be one standard size.
And it seemed to these special advisory guys
That the standard that ought to be henceforth applied
Was ten and a half long by eight inches wide.

And so it has been for the last sixty years.
Standard, but not too efficient, one fears.
For the rest of the world, when it sent out a letter,
Thought eight and a half by eleven was better.
So sizes were different, depending on source,
And the envelopes had to be different, of course.
And the folders in which certain papers would sit
Would have to be different or they wouldn't fit.
And the cabinets into which folders were piled
So the papers inside could be sorted and filed.

It affected procedures in numerous ways.
Photocopy machines had not one, but two trays.
At the start of this decade, this seemed such a pity
That Washington set up another committee
To study the problem and measure the pinch
Produced by the shortage of this half an inch.
So the panel got busy and hired a staff
To see if eight inches by ten and a half
Ought to be changed to more closely conform
To the rest of the world and its paper-shape norm.

Uncle Sam uses paper in quantities great,
And the flow of that paper seems not to abate.
More paper than most people's wildest of dreams;
Each year about 2.8 million reams.
One-point-four billion sheets—enough paper, I think,
To drive any sensible person to drink.
And in sending out stuff, what they often will do
When they run out of space is to start a page two.
And the taxpayers' pennies quite seldom one pinches
By using sheets eight-by-ten-point-five inches.
It must seem to a bureaucrat something like heaven
To write on an eight and a half by eleven.

So rejoice, everybody, and know that reform
Has come to the government's paper-size norm.

Never let it be said that those Washington folks
Are unwilling to change, are intransigent blokes.
They've been doing it wrong, there's no reason to doubt it,
But, by George, they're now doing something about it.
It is wasteful and costly and also inflationary
When bureaucrats have to use funny-sized stationery.

Memorable Conversions: Long Island Chapter

Because of rising oil rates,
A man on Long Island, in Roslyn Estates,
Decided the moment had now come to pass
To convert from such oil to natural gas.
It seemed like a sensible move he could make,
And it might have been, too, but for one small mistake.

Jay Rosenfield lives out in Roslyn Estates
In a very nice house, but it seems that the fates
Weren't good to the house, for they happened to bring
To the address concerned an unfortunate thing.
Jay Rosenfield tired of paying for oil;
The oil bill figures just made his blood boil.
So he thought of a seemingly useful alternative:
Natural gas, as a substitute burnative.

He looked up his heating firm, gave them a call,
And had them come over and please to install
A new heating system, with natural gas.
And they came and they did it all, simply first class.
And they took out the oil tank, an old furnace system.
With the new rig they put in, why, nobody missed 'em.

And all this improving of which I now speak
Was done in the Rosenfield home just last week.
At the end of which time, we might possibly mention,
Jay Rosenfield left to attend a convention.
He's been out in Las Vegas, his relatives say.
So when what happened happened, poor Jay was away.

An oil delivery man, Daniel Dutton,
Did not get the word, and so didn't know nuttin'

About the new system, although there's no doubt
It was his firm that took the old oil tank out.
He drove up in a tank truck. You know about those.
And he unscrewed the filler cap, dropped in the hose,
And proceeded to empty the oil in the truck
Into Rosenfield's basement—a bit of bad luck.

Out of the tank truck the heating oil flowed;
Through the hose to the basement, the fuel oil rode.
Three hundred and forty-five gallons or more.
Why, the oil meter clicked, keeping excellent score.
The oil in the basement had no place to go.
It just flooded the place, but the man didn't know
Until he realized he'd pumped in, and therefore had sold,
A whole lot more oil than the old tank would hold.

And to make matters worse, this delivery bloke
Had this terrible feeling he also smelled smoke.
What had happened inside was the new pilot light
Had caused the pool of oil to burn, to ignite.
And now Mr. Dutton had feelings quite dire,
For the Rosenfield house, at that point, was on fire.

The fire department arrived on the scene,
But the smoke was quite thick, if you know what I mean.
And when Dutton explained what his call was about,
They went right to work and the fire was put out.
But the whole basement ceiling, the whole kitchen floor,
Aren't at all what they were any more.
The place is described as quite damaged, substantially.
It's bound to cost somebody plenty, financially.

It was something nobody had anticipated.
Whose fault all this was will be roundly debated.
Somehow from Dutton a key fact was hid.
It shouldn't have happened, yet somehow it did.

It's a shame, people say, that nobody foresaw.
If such things can happen, there should be a law.
There's already a law, folks. Yes, that much I know.
It was written by Murphy . . . a long time ago.

How Not to Succeed in the Banking Business

On Staten Island, there's a bank branch manager, I fear,
Who has suffered a reversal in his managing career.
He put his trust in someone, though now he wonders why,
Who said he was an agent of the fabled FBI.

A hundred thousand dollars he turned over, it is said,
And there's an assistant manager whose face is rather red.
The Citibank commercials say, "The Citi Never Sleeps."
It's a never-sleeping giant bank, a bank that plays for keeps,
With assets that are staggering, impressive as can be;
More money, folks, than you or I will likely ever see.

A conservative establishment whose people, as a rule,
Are careful with the money. They're not easy men to fool.
But yesterday the phone rang in a Staten Island branch,
And the branch assistant manager, his face began to blanch
When he heard the caller's voice and what the caller had to
    say.
It was not at all the ideal way to start a banker's day.

The man explained that he was with the FBI, you see,
And was calling to inquire whether there might chance to be
A bomb out in the vestibule beneath a banker's table.
The manager ran out to look as fast as he was able,
And sure enough, he found an object ominous and dire—
What looked like sticks of dynamite bound up with coils of
    wire.
And a timing mechanism that would make a banker sick.
A box he saw connected, yes, and he could hear it tick.

He ran back to the telephone, reported what he'd seen.
The agent on the other end seemed quick and cool and keen.
You trust someone who seems to know, and this man surely
    knew.
And he said, "Assistant manager, this is what you do.

Do not touch the ticking bomb, but you must right away
Follow my instructions. Do exactly what I say.
Take the money, all the money, in the night-deposit box."
The branch assistant manager had keys to all the locks.

"Put the money in a garbage bag," said the telephone G-man,
"And go outside and wait there for a gray and unmarked van.
An agent in gray uniform, a driver straight and steady,
And you be on the sidewalk with the money bagged and
    ready.
Don't hesitate, don't question, please. The time is very slim.
When the driver of the van pulls up, you give the bag to
    him."

The branch assistant manager, obedient and bold,
Did what he believed was right, did just as he was told.
He quickly put the money in a plastic garbage bag.
He knew the bomb was ticking; he could not afford to lag.

The van pulled up exactly as the caller said it would,
And the branch assistant manager out on a sidewalk stood
And he handed up the money, and the van just pulled away.
A professional and very neatly executed play.
The poor assistant manager, when a certain time passed by,
Decided to fill in the cops about the FBI.
So he went back inside the bank and telephoned the police.
The bomb squad came right over—they were down the road
    a piece.

And they quickly then discovered, through some cautious steps
    they take
That the ticking bomb inside was just a phony, just a fake,
A harmless combination of some parts of clocks and spares,
And what looked like sticks of dynamite were really only
    flares.

And furthermore, on checking with the FBI, they learned
That the agent was a phony. So the Citibank got burned.
A hundred thousand dollars to the fellow in the van,
And there's one assistant manager, a sadder, wiser man.
Police say they don't have a clue to solve the case, they fear.
"Cut-and-dried right now. Looks like somebody had a hocus-
    pocus here."

Followup Story on the White House Guards and Their Epauletic Fit

Sometimes you hear stories in the news. The who, what, where, and when
That never got followed up on, and you wonder what happened then.
Whatever became of what's-his-name, and where did he go, and how?
And whatever happened to so-and-so, and what is he doing now?

But some of these stories never die, this morning I'm here to say.
Nor are they like old soldiers—they do not just fade away.
And this week they moved a story on Associated Press
That sparked a nostalgic memory, and I said to myself, "Ah, yes!"

It had to do with the White House and the trappings that adjoin,
But now it was out of Iowa and the dateline read Des Moines.
Once upon a recent time, though it still makes some people wince,
The White House guards appeared dressed up like the cast of *The Student Prince.*

It was back in the early seventies, in a Richard Nixon year,
When the guards turned out in something that looked like *Der Rosenkavalier.*
Mr. Nixon had been to Belgium, to NATO and thereabouts,
And noticed the Prussian uniforms that now and then Brussels sprouts.

And when he got home, he ordered some, had a hundred and fifty made,

With double-breasted tunics, and with golden shoulder braid.
With helmets of visored vinyl, with buttons of shining brass.
Mr. Nixon thought it would dress things up, give the place a
    little class.

With the shining vinyl, the shining buttons, the tunics of
    gleaming white,
The guards did make an impression. It's true they were quite
    a sight.
The very first time they wore them turned out to be the last.
As traditions go this came in and then went out real fast.

Instead of providing the dignity, the spectacle and such,
The outfits inspired amusement, and were ridiculed so much
That after the very first wearing out there on the White
    House lawn
The Ruritanian doorman suits were quietly withdrawn.

They had cost ten thousand dollars, but were that very day
Rendered no longer operative, and were folded and put away
Into a government warehouse, kept under lock and key,
With no one around to look at them, nobody allowed to see.

The years passed, went by quite fast, and most of us forgot.
But does Washington ever forget such things? The fact is it
    does not.
The Secret Service would happily have given the things away,
But did not have such authority, or that's what the lawyers say.

So they stayed in the locked-up closet, just gathering dust for
    years—
Interesting, admittedly, but embarrassing souvenirs.
Opera companies wanted them. Requests were rejected since
Perhaps it was feared they'd really be used by the cast of *The
    Student Prince*.

They became simply government surplus. What the GSA
    then did

Was put the uniforms up for sale—simply offer them up for
    bid.
The states by law got first crack at them, got to offer a little
    coin.
And one of the winning bids, it seems, came from somebody
    in Des Moines.

Tom Roller's in charge of the state's surplus stock,
And thirty-two uniforms put up on the block
Are his to do with as he will. And will wonders never cease?
He will offer them to high school bands for five or ten bucks
    apiece.

A fellow named Jack Warner, not of Hollywood fame,
But the Washington Jack Warner—Secret Service is his
    game—
Once said of the famous outfits, "They'd be great for operatic
    romances. . . .
I think, if we were to sum it up, we would say they were
    probably just too much pomp for the circumstances."

The rest of your life
Is about to begin.
That's good reason for putting
A holiday in. (A Holiday Inn?)

Special Days

Ho Ho Ho My Foot

Among the many benefits of Christmas we receive
Is the widget we assemble for the kids on Christmas Eve.
All it takes is being handy—which I'm afraid I ain't—
A screwdriver and a hammer and the patience of a saint.

Christmas is a merry time, all filled with peace and joy,
And it's eagerly awaited by each little girl and boy.
For when it's Christmas Eve, as any kid can well explain,
    dear,
Santa does his thing with toys, his ride with sleigh and
    reindeer.

And he brings stuff down the chimney and he leaves it by the
    tree,
If that's the way it really was, it would be okay with me.
But last night, when all our little kids were nestled in their
    beds,
With the mandatory sugarplums all dancing in their heads,

My wife and I got busy and we filled the Christmas soxes
And dug into the closet and pulled out a lot of boxes.
Kathleen, Winston, also Annie, safe and snug in bed were
    nestled.
And 'twas then with Holly Hobby Dolly Highchair that I
    wrestled.

Just a simple little project, or so it seemed to me.
All it took was a screwdriver and an engineer's degree.
It comes in many pieces, some of plastic, some of wood.
I won't tell you what they were, although I'd do that if I
    could.

There were fronts and sides, a footrest, and some armrests
    and a tray.
And I looked at the directions to see what they might say.

They referred me to a plastic bag in which were many screws.
You never know at that point just which one of those you'll
   lose.

They come in several sizes, I am sorry to report,
Which means you're bound to use one that's too long, perhaps
   too short.
And then, a little later on, if you're still holding steady,
You'll find you need a certain screw which you have used
   already.

But it's Christmas Eve, and so, without delay, you duly start,
With carols on the stereo and Christmas in your heart.
And you chuckle just a little bit and whistle while you work.
And pretty soon you realize you've been a sort of jerk.

For the sides you screwed into the chair, attached right to the
   seat
(Although they fit quite readily and look precise and neat),
There is a certain something here that you already lack,
For one side faces front, you see, the other faces back.

So, the screws with which you patiently had started in to
   screw
You have to start all over. You begin then to undo,
And you mutter very quietly, so no one else can hear,
A little phrase of greeting, of well-being and good cheer

As you turn the little dolly chair, where now without a doubt
You're ready to proceed, but upside down and inside out.
And the holes that they pre-drilled so all of this would be a
   cinch
Miss lining up together by a quarter of an inch.

And you see that when you've done step four as nice as it can
   be,
You've got to do it over, since you failed to do step three.

Flap A does not match up at all with what they call Tab B,
And both of those must interlock before you touch Flange C.

The head of the screwdriver is off by just a bit,
And so, into the little notch it doesn't want to fit.
It slips as you are turning just a fraction of an inch
And gives your index finger an excruciating pinch.

Whereupon you utter—and you do so then and there—
Your opinion of the outfit that produced the bloody chair.
Whoever would imagine, whoever would believe,
One could come so far apart on just one Christmas Eve?

But now it's Christmas morning, and under the tree
Are the presents. And the children are glad as can be.
One thing I'm proudest of (see it right there?)
Is that slightly off-center dolly highchair.

Lucky Seven

There are seven saintly virtues and seven deadly sins
And seven, if you roll it in a crap game, sometimes wins.
There are seven wonders of the world, and seven-year itches,
And seven dwarfs, as Snow White learned, can trouble
    wicked witches.
The reason I've composed these lines of roughly rhyming
    couplets
About septuagenarians and folks who are septuplets,
Is the fact that circumstances, destiny, and fate
Have conspired to make this day, today, a heavy seven date.

If you believe the number seven is for you propitious
You're not alone, for many are in that way superstitious.
It's 7/7/77 (day and month and year)
And people all around the world will take that fact, I fear,
To mean that something special is likely to occur
With very lucky overtones, for him, I mean, or her.

In New York City on this day, inside the Taft Hotel,
They're planning now to celebrate in certain ways as well,
With movies and with dances, a dance of seven veils.
The Taft believes that on this day they'll do quite well with
    sales,
With a prize each seven minutes—seven dollars cash, and
    others,
And a movie they'll be showing, *Seven Brides for Seven
    Brothers.*
They say that should you care to come, they'll be prepared for
    havin' you,
For the Taft's address is 777 Seventh Avenue.

This seventh day and month, on this most sevenish of years
Has sevens everywhere you look. They're coming out our
    ears.
Folks are getting married on this seventh of July;

Someday, seven years from now, they well may wonder
   why. . . .
Post offices around the world this morning, it appears,
Expect a flood of business, for but once each hundred years
Does the postmark read the way this does (a nice quadruple
   seven).
It's true all day in Malibu, in Greenwich, and in Devon.

There's a baby in Australia, in Adelaide they say,
Born the seventh minute of the seventh hour today.
The boy, incidentally, arrived just seven days late,
And seven pounds and seven ounces was the baby's weight

Ken Wallace is a parachutist, he's from Illinois,
Who always has been something of a superstitious boy.
And Wallace plans to mark today, this luckiest of dates,
With seven jumps in seven hours, in seven different states.

But if you set store in numbers, remember this is true:
What's lucky for the other guy may not be so for you.
For superstition cuts both ways about the number seven;
It's popular in hell, they say, as well as up in heaven.
And should you break a mirror, I'm afraid you would be
   stuck.
For everybody knows that that means seven years' bad luck.
And should you bet the seventh horse in the seventh race—
And I'm certain here and there that that will be the case—
You'll play the horse at any odds and then you'll pray to
   heaven
That when they're off you'll cheer him on with: "Come on,
   number seven!"
The seventh day and month, the seventh race and seventh
   horse,
A natural (you're bound to think). What happens, though, of
   course,
What well might be on such a day, in such a seventh race,
The seventh horse will finish for you . . . right in seventh
   place.

One Set of Scrapped New Year's Resolutions

I resolve that in the coming year of 1979
In any broadcast of the news that happens to be mine
The snow will always be just snow. Whatever is in store
I promise not to call it "fluffy white stuff" any more.
I resolve that in the coming year no cigarette I'll smoke.
That sounds like something very wise, but here's the little
    joke:
I never have been the least inclined to smoke a cigarette,
And I'm not about to start now if I haven't done so yet.

I'll keep out of all those discos, will not dance the latest dance.
There's no way I'll go back on that. There's not the slightest
    chance,
For I do not look in any way at all like John Travolta,
And the music they play, anyway, to me is quite revolta.

I promise not to jog this year. I tried that once before,
And vowed that should I live I would not do it any more.
I resolve that I will never run when walking could be tried.
I resolve that I will never walk if I can get a ride.
I'll never stand when I can sit. I hate standing around.
Nor will I sit, if there's any way I could be lying down.
I'll renounce all forms of broccoli, and cauliflower too.
And kidney pie's another thing I'll readily eschew.

I promise not to promise things. That's good, for there and
    then
It cancels out the sense of resolutions one through ten.
But I am willing, nonetheless, to here highly resolve
That none of the great problems of the world I'll try to solve.
And though I'll point my finger at the leaders of the day,
And tell what wrong they've done and what I'd do if I were
    they,
I promise to be helpful and be free with my advice;
To hold back would be selfish. That would not be very nice.

I resolve that in the coming year I always will be frank.
And if that stings a little, you have honesty to thank.
I'll encourage everyone to work in sunshine or in showers.
I'm crazy about work. Why, I could look at it for hours.
I take the pledge that when I can, I'll pour myself a drink.
It ought to be an interesting year, don't you think?
And in whatever poems that I possibly may plan,
I resolve not to get hung up in such piddling little
  inconsequential and unimportant details, such as
  whether or not they scan.

The Return of the Grinch

The season of Christmas was meant to be merry,
But this time it seems to be not awfully very.
Somewhat less jollity, feasting, and bonhomie,
Due to the state of the Western economy.
Who is responsible? Who is the Scrooge?
Who is doing this very un-Christmas trick huge?
I say that the signs are quite visibly clear
As to who is the villain at Christmas this year.

"Elementary," I say, as might old Sherlock Holmes,
It isn't the work of the Zurich-type gnomes—
The solution, I tell you, is really a cinch:
The one who's at fault is that wicked old Grinch
With respect and apologies to Dr. Seuss,
The clues are right there in the day's breaking neuss.

Shopping around for some Christmassy books
And turning the pages for Christmassy looks,
I encounter again for the umpty-umpth time
The delightful Seuss story in pictures and rhyme
Of how the old Grinch early one Christmas day
Didn't like Christmas, so he took it away.
And so Christmas, which Whoville had liked such a lot,
Was removed by the Grinch, because he sure did not.

The Grinch hated Christmas, as Seuss made quite clear,
And he made hating Christmas a lifelong career.
He hated the whole thing, the whole Christmas season
For some very dubious personal reason.
It could be his head wasn't screwed on just right.
It could be, perhaps, that his shoes were too tight.
But Seuss thought the most likely reason of all
May have been that his heart was two sizes too small.

So one night he descended and broke all the laws
And acted the part of an un-Santa Claus.
He dressed up as Santa and raided the Whos
And emptied their stockings as part of his ruse.
And then up the chimney he shoved the Whos' tree
Did the Grinch. . . . Not a very nice fellow was he.
He even made off with a lovely roast beast
That the Whos had intended to have for their feast.

Now, with that kind of modus for his operandi,
It seems to me simple as eating a candy.
The Grinch must be doing his thing once again
As he did once before down in Whoville back when.
Only this time he went to old Washington town,
Found the Commerce Department, the chimney went down,
And, dressed in his very same Santa Claus raiments,
Adjusted the rates and the balance of payments.

To the Labor Department he flew like a flash,
To the Bureau of Labor Statistics so rash,
And, using red ink from his little Grinch cup,
Made employment go down, unemployment go up.
Then the Grinch flew away to the city Detroit
And he cackled, "Ho ho. This is going to hoit."

He had said not a word, but the Grinch, like a jerk,
Proceeded to put people there out of work.
And he changed all the price tags in every store.
In each case made them much higher than they were before.
So outrageously high everybody would mind them
And he hid the WIN buttons so no one could find them.

He moved down to Wall Street amidst all the moans.
And greased up the skids on the grinchy Dow Jones.
But what happened in Whoville, you folks may recall,
Was that even the Grinch, though his heart was too small,

Had to admit when it came to the day
That Christmas occurred, that it came anyway.

And his heart grew three sizes, and he came unbending,
And the Seuss story ends with a nice happy ending.
And today, if we only would just realize
Whatever your own, or the Grinch's, heart size
That Christmas is coming, whatever we do
And a year that is open and ready and new.
Who can say how the story will go for the rest of it?
Christmas is coming! Let's all make the best of it.

Friday the Thirteenth

Superstitious? A lot of people are, all over the world. Even the Russians. UPI's man in Moscow writes this morning that if a Russian hears a buzzing in his ears, he will ask you to guess which ear is buzzing (the left or the right), and if you guess correctly, he will get his wish. If you guess wrong, he believes he won't. No wonder it's so hard to negotiate with the Russians.

Circus people are superstitious about a lot of things. Circus historian C. P. Fox says there are many portents of disaster in the circus, including the color yellow, peanut shells in the dressing room, somebody knitting in the first few rows, or a watch that stops at either 8:00 A.M. or 8:00 P.M. Fox says it is also a circus tradition that if you see a cross-eyed person, you should spit in a hat.

Mariners are extremely superstitious about Friday the thirteenth. John Grindle of Belfast, Maine, has written about the wreck of the *Solferino*, a ship that drew thirteen feet of water, in which the crew, while killing rats below decks before sailing on a Friday the thirteenth, accidentally killed a black cat. Sounds like trouble! And sure enough, there was trouble. Mutiny and, finally, shipwreck. Grindle says the *Solferino* and all hands were lost.

Well, today we have a story on the Associated Press about the prelate and former exorcist by the name of Monsignor Corrado Balducci, who has been studying the so-called Prophecies of Saint Malechi—an ancient list of mottoes for each pope.

Malechi was a twelfth-century Irish monk and archbishop. The so-called prophecies are believed by many scholars not to be his, but forgeries from the sixteenth century. Nevertheless, Monsignor Balducci's commentaries on them appear in the latest issue of the Vatican weekly, *Osservatore de la Dominica*. He says Malechi's motto for the next pope, the one that's about to be named, is "*De Labori Soli,*" or, "Of the Fatigue of the Sun." Balducci says at least one possible interpretation of this is that there will be some great cataclysm, which he says would most likely be World War III.

Of course, that is not the only possible cataclysm. Astronomers at the Hayden Planetarium in New York City, a few years back, made a compendium of the awful stuff that could possibly happen, including (and this is just a partial list): the earth might suddenly become volcanically active and boil over; the whole universe could collapse; we could collide with a black hole—one of those areas in space so dense that not even light can escape from it; we could collide with a swarm of meteoroids, although meteoroid swarms are relatively scarce out there; we could collide with a comet, which would not necessarily mean the end of the world, but could sure do some serious damage to the city. (The South Bronx already looks as if it's been hit by a comet.) Or, the moon could fall in on us. The astronomers say that's not at all farfetched; in fact, sooner or later it probably will. But not for a long time. And inevitably, the astronomers say, the sun will get old, poop out—*de labori soli,* so to speak—turn into a giant red star, engulf Mercury and Venus, and make things so hot for us here on earth that lead will melt.

But the forecast for this is that is will happen about five billion years from now. No sense getting all upset about it today. Unless, of course, you are overwhelmed by superstition.

Jack Douglas, the philosopher, tells us that the dwarf French artist Henri de Toulouse-Lautrec was extremely superstitious. He would never, under any circumstances, walk under a black cat.

Monday

When we get the day off on the Fourth of July,
There's no need to ask or to contemplate why.
We do it because you and I are descendants
Of people who that day declared independence.
And Christmas is Christmas, and on the New Year
The old year is gone and the new one is here.

And Thanksgiving Day we all stay home from workey
And feast on the trimmings that go with the turkey
To thank the Almighty for all that he gave.
It's a fine and commendable way to behave.
But it's always on Thursday, which regular break
Caused some folks to think (which can be a mistake).

And here's what they thought: They thought, "Just suppose
    one day
We had all our holidays fall on a Monday."
So they set Labor Day in the month of September—
The first Monday thereof, so we all would remember.
And then we'd have three whole days off in a row
With time, if we wanted, to take off and go.

It wasn't a holiday marking some date,
Some birthday or some great occasion of state.
It was simply a Monday, a chance, we were told,
To enjoy the late summer before it got cold.
And to honor the workingman early each fall
By not having very much working at all.

The principle thereby established, of course,
Developed its own irresistible force.
And soon enough people discovered the fact
That caused them (apparently) sometimes to act
As if working on Monday were awful and cruel.
Blue Monday, they called it. And sometimes they'd fool

The boss into thinking they'd just fallen ill
With a sickness for which there is no cure and no pill.
Better to plead to a sin of omission
Than to show up for work in a weekend condition.
Absentee rates run higher that day,
Or so the statistical histories say.

So they set certain holidays off to one side,
And these did they then subsequently decide
To put on a Monday. Yes, that was their plot.
Whether those events fell on a Monday or not.
And that is why we've made George Washington's birthday
A movable feast, like Thanksgiving or Earth Day.

February fifteenth, back in '71,
When all this moving-around business was begun.
To the twenty-first then, back in '72.
Poor old George didn't know, I am sure, what to do.
It moved back to the nineteenth in '73.
It all seems just a little confusing to me.

On the eighteenth they had it in '74.
All this moving around was a bit of a bore.
And this time around, it is Feb. seventeen.
Now, tell me, what does such a date mean?
True, to avoid the predictable slams
They've compounded the error by adding new shams.

It's not Washington's Birthday, they'd surely say,
We're off because this, this is Presidents' Day.
Not George's or Abe's. Not Gerald's or Dick's.
Not Lyndon's or Jack's. It would just make you sick.
But an omnibus President's Monday day off.
An unspecified President—but do not scoff—

For though it may be just a bit of a ruse day,
You don't have to go back to work until Tuesday.

What does it mean? What does it mean?
This national holiday, Feb. seventeen?
It means that they will not deliver your mail.
That you can count upon. Yes, without fail.

And though Washington's Birthday has gone off the rail,
They'll still have those Washington's big birthday sales.
But you better have cash, because, well, what the heck,
The banks are all closed and you can't cash a check.
But, stockholders, smile, there is no need to frown
For the market is closed, and it will not go down.

People are awful
They give me the blues
But without them there wouldn't
Be much in the news.

People

Why Not the Worst?

There were many things this morning from which we had to
    choose,
But we picked a little story in the New York *Daily News*.
It is all about a criminal, and really such a pity:
The worst, most unprofessional pickpocket in the city.

His name is Gregory Gatson, and his age is twenty-four,
And the cops have now arrested him some fifty times or more.
Such dreadful notoriety young Gatson never sought.
But he brought it on himself, because he keeps on getting
    caught.

His manual dexterity is that of many thumbs.
His front teeth are all missing. When he smiles you see his
    gums.
Someone punched him in the mouth, you see, and did it with
    such force
The teeth came out. We'll tell you all about that in due
    course.

If you take up picking pockets as a livelihood, you see,
It's important that you have a touch as light as it can be.
You must move with anonymity, with grace and poise and
    stealth,
If you choose that risky method of accumulating wealth.

You must be slick and lightning-quick each time you sidle by,
And walking proof the hand, indeed, is quicker than the eye.
Your victims must be unaware of what is going on.
And by the time they realize it, you have come and gone.

But Gregory is not at all that slippery sort of guy.
His stubby hands are slower than most anybody's eye.
And as he picks a pocket, Gregory Gatson's touch is such
That anyone would notice it—that heavy-handed clutch.

And lifting someone's wallet or removing someone's purse,
It's hard to think that anyone could possibly be worse.
One woman that he tried to rob shoved Gregory away.
"He tried to open up my purse, but couldn't," I am told.
"My daughter does it all the time. She's only five years old."

One day a big policeman stood in Nedick's hot dog stand.
The cop in full cop's uniform, I hope you understand.
When in came Gregory Gatson, looking nervously around,
Looking for a chance to strike, a chance that he soon found.

For when someone pulled a dollar out in payment for a frank,
Gatson jumped in front of him and gave the bill a yank.
Whereupon he felt, in turn, a tapping on his shoulder.
Gatson somehow doesn't seem to learn as he gets older.
The police have learned to watch him, though, it's easy as can
   be.
His file is number 3470790Z.

The policeman at the Nedick's stand, who carried out the
   law,
Described it as the poorest stealing job he ever saw.
He's earned some sort of record, if indeed such files are kept.
Of all the working pickpockets, he's the most inept.

It was only two weeks later, the same officer would hear
From a nearby subway station such an awful scream of fear
That he ran down to the station. What he saw there made
   him gulp:
A large man in a sportcoat beating Gatson to a pulp.

The gentleman was angry, for he said this little jerk
Had tried to steal his wallet while he traveled home from
   work.
And the two of them were on the ground, Greg Gatson was
   beneath,
It was in this encounter that he lost a few front teeth.

When Gatson used to be arrested, the thing that he'd do then
Was to claim it wasn't him at all, but his twin brother,
    Glenn.
And sure enough, there is a twin; Glenn Gatson is his name.
And Glenn and Gregory Gatson did indeed look much the
    same.

But now, you see, it happens that no longer is the case.
The two of them are quite a lot alike there in the face.
Till they open up their mouths, and the excuse is shot—
For one of them has all his teeth. The other one has not.

When would-be victims testify about a toothless schnook,
Police just shake their heads and sigh. They know just where
    to look.
As professional pickpocket, poor Gatson lacks in style.
And now he must remember, while he's working, not to smile.

Think How Peaceful Life Will Be When You Reach the Age of 103

In Eastern Maryland living there
Is a gentleman named Jimmy Fair.
He's not as young as he used to be,
For his age is now one hundred and three.
But still quite active, be it understood—
Perhaps too active for his own good.
Which could be one of the reasons why
"Buzzard" is what friends call the guy.

He was born June sixth, so the records say,
Which means that his birthday was yesterday.
The real name of Buzzard is Jimmy Fair,
And Eastern Shore folks say he's been living there
For quite a while, and was staying with
Another fellow named Randolph Smith.

Now, this past April they had a fight
Over who was wrong and who was right.
Though we don't know what it was all about,
It was quite a battle, there is no doubt.

And to make a long story short,
Jimmy Fair ended up yesterday in court,
For police said old Buzzard was at fault.
He was charged with battery and assault.

And Randolph Smith had evidence, which is
In his scalp were thirteen stitches.
For no good reason, complainant said,
Buzzard Smith had bopped him right on the head.

And a piece of pipe, said Randolph Smith,
Was the weapon James Fair had hit Smith with.
Now, a metal pipe on the cranial parts
Can do great damage—it really smarts.

Even when wielded, the court was told,
By a man one hundred and three years old.
"Not guilty" is how old Buzzard pleaded.
He only did it because he needed
To bop the fellow and ring his chime
Because Smith was choking him at the time.

The judge was Judge William Dunbar Gould,
And this was the finding that Judge Gould ruled:
On assault and battery, as depicted,
He found Fair guilty. He stood convicted.

One year in jail, that might have ended it,
But Gould gave the sentence and then suspended it.
Two years' probation Fair must stay.
Two years, that is, starting yesterday.
To straighten out he must therefore strive.
He'll be closely watched till he's one-oh-five.

Now, what must have made the old fellow whine,
The judge also slapped him with a fine.
A hundred dollars he had to pay
For doing the thing that he'd done that day,
For assaulting the gent he was living with,
To wit, the aforementioned Randolph Smith.

And another thing at the same time ruled
By the district judge, William Dunbar Gould,
Was that Fair cannot live with Smith any more,
Lest they scuffle again as they did before.
The Buzzard has got to move out of there.
That's the court ruling. And fair is fair.

Jimmy Fair, known as Buzzard, now says that he
Will remember the day he turned one hundred and three,
And the lecture he got and the hundred-buck fine,
And he says that he'll try to keep in line.
But that won't be easy, to tell you the truth,
For old Buzzard is still an impetuous youth.

Chiang Ching Was a Mean Old Thing

In this country, we get to make up our own minds about people in public life. At least we get to hear what they say and we get to hear what people say about them. That is not true elsewhere. When the government controls the press (as it does in most of the world), the opinions you get about anything and anybody *are* necessarily those of the management—the management of the country, that is.

In the People's Republic of China, for example, we know only what we hear about Chiang Ching, the widow of Chairman Mao Tse-tung. We used to hear only good things about her. How pure was her zeal, how deep her devotion to her wonderful and great husband.

Well, now, of course, that place is under new management. And from everything we can find out about her now, it seems that Chiang Ching is really a rather despicable sort. In fact, every day the Chinese press has some new outrage to report about some perfectly awful thing she did. So one might now reasonably conclude that Chiang Ching is probably the worst person in the world. A more rotten person you would not encounter anywhere.

In China today, poets and authors and artists and songwriters are busy turning out stuff about Mao Tse-tung's widow and her Gang of Four—how unspeakably mean and selfish and immoral and wasteful and disloyal and thoroughly hateful they are, and how terrific Mao's successor, Hua Kuo-feng, is.

The following verse is not actually translated from the Chinese, but it might well have been. All of the accusations contained herein are accusations that actually have been made in the last few weeks against Chiang Ching.

Chiang Ching
Is a mean old thing
And she had a Gang of Four.
And China is very lucky
That she's carrying on no more.

Chiang Ching
Did chaos bring
Whenever she was around.
Her deportment was such
It was just too much,
The current regime has found.

She was constantly badgering Mao Tse-tung,
And nagging him all the time,
And asking for money.
It wasn't funny.
How she treated him was a crime.

She liked to gamble, and liked to drink,
And often watched foreign flicks.
She wanted to play
The part, they say,
Of a prostitute turning tricks.

She disrupted the people so very much
They were forced to make mistakes,
Resulting in unnecessary deaths
When the earth had its recent quakes.

Old Chiang Ching
Was a wicked old thing,
And a wicked old thing was she.
She plotted how to kill Chairman Mao,
She and her partners three.

Old Chiang Ching
And her Gang of Four
Made plots against Mao Tse-tung,
And they might succeed
Were it not for the deeds
Of the wonderful Hua Kuo-feng.

It is he who exposed them for what they were:
Four terrible running dogs.

In the people's machine of bureaucracy
They put bubble gum in the cogs.

During artillery practice one day,
The Chinese army to teach,
Chiang Ching had them stop
While she went clip-clop,
Collecting shells on the beach.

The Chairman's wife
Was a source of strife
Of many a Red Guard brawl.
But now she's discredited,
Posters have said it.
The handwriting's on the wall.

She was playing poker when Mao died.
And how do you think she'd feel?
When they told her to rush,
All she said was, "Hush!
This is poker. Shut up and deal!"

It's hard to see how Chairman Mao
Continued to be so kind
To someone so terribly mean to him.
Apparently, love is blind.

Bedfellows make strange politics
And politics strange bedfellows.
And stranger yet
Are the things you get
When the Chairman becomes a dead fellow.

Old Chiang Ching
Is a wicked thing,
And her deeds are not forgotten.
She was once a saint,
But now she ain't.
How could she be so rotten?

A Matter of Principle and Man's Inalienable Cookie

Over the weekend, Ken Harsh was arrested,
And an issue of law may now therefore be tested:
Whether one may speak out, or must button one's lip
And turn over one's cookie—one's chocolate chip.

In Norfolk, Virginia, not far from a marsh,
Something happened this weekend to one Kenneth Harsh.
An ex-Naval officer, not looking for a fight,
"My wife and I went to the Military Circle Mall shopping
    center on Saturday night."

They decided, when finished, a movie to see.
Agatha was playing, it happened to be.
While she shopped, he bought tickets, for those two are not
    rookies.
"While waiting for the tickets I just happened to notice this
    little cookie place that opened there, so I bought two
    cookies."

Little did he realize fate now had him in its grip.
"From the Original Great American Chocolate Chip Cookie
    Company. Chocolate chip."
Who would think this would become a confrontation in
    someone's life?
"Anyway, I bought two cookies. One for myself and one for
    my wife."

Harsh knew he might have to wait awhile, since waiting for
    one's wife to finish shopping can be a bit of a joke.
"So I walked up to the concession stand and bought a box of
    popcorn and a Coke."
He sipped the Coke, while waiting there. Just something to
    do.
And he ate the box of popcorn. Harsh was slightly hungry,
    too.

"And then the cookie, and then I saved one of the cookies for
    my wife."
To save one's wife a cookie shouldn't cause a lot of strife.
But she must have snacked on something, while on her
    shopping roam.
"She said no, she didn't want the cookie, and I said, 'All
    right. Well, I'll just save it and you can have it when we
    get home.'"

So they walked into the theater with the cookie in a bag,
And an usher there on duty, with an eye that did not flag,
Spotted something and swung into action, if you can believe,
"And the usher came over and said that I would have to give
    him my cookie or leave."

Kenneth Harsh was now in trouble, as he'd know before too
    long.
"And I told him I wasn't going to give him my cookie, and I
    wasn't going to leave the theater because I hadn't done
    anything wrong."
And the manager came over, and he made the ultimatum:
He couldn't bring cookies in because, well, he just might have
    ate 'em
Instead of eating theater food, and that would be a sin.
"I'd already bought the popcorn. It was just an unusual
    situation to be in."

A classic battle fate was weaving.
"I had paid for my ticket and I wasn't leaving."
Mrs. Harsh was mortified; such circumstances shame her.
"She was there at the time, of course, telling me to give them
    the cookie, and not wanting me to create a scene. And I
    can't blame her."

Kenneth Harsh does love his wife, did not want to offend her,
But his principles and cookie he could not now surrender.
So two guards were called to settle things, which they did
    without a doubt.
They took our hero by the arms and escorted him out.

They turned him over to police. Now pretty bad things
   looked.
"And then they took me downtown to the First Precinct,
   where I was booked."
Kenneth Harsh was dealt with harshly, as the warrant on
   him showed.
"I am charged with violation of Section 3117 of the City
   Code."

He would not give up his cookie. Put that motto on his
   banner.
But the warrant put it otherwise.
"Did act in a tumultuous manner."
With the court now Harsh has posted a hundred-dollar bond,
Of such trouble and attention, Kenneth Harsh is not too fond.
"I wish it hadn't happened," is what Kenneth Harsh now
   grumbles,
And if he loses out, well, that's the way the cookie crumbles.

He's Okay, She's Okay

Thomas Harris is okay,
Okay in quite a special way,
The book he wrote some years ago
Did rather well, as you may know.
About ten million copies sold—
Or that's the number we are told.
When all that many books you sell
You do okay. You do quite well.

Dr. Harris and his wife
Are both okay, enjoying life.
He's okay. She's okay.
They're both okay, or so they say.
Among the things that they are doing
Is going into court and suing.
Suing someone who, they say
Said Harris wasn't so okay.

They're mad because this fellow said
That Harris was deceased. Was dead.
The Harrises' attorneys say
That when you're dead, you're not okay.
That quite the opposite is true,
And that is why they've filed to sue.

Harris says it isn't so
He killed himself two years ago.
This lawsuit filed, this legal fight
Proves Harris is alive, all right.

Over nineteen million dollars in damages they claim
For the harm they say was done the reputation and the name
Of the Harrises, whose famous book, *I'm OK—You're OK*
Has sold ten million copies and is selling still today.

Larry Tomczak, an evangelist, is charged with having said
That Thomas Harris killed himself and therefore now is
  dead.
The people still were following the precepts of his book,
Even though the author's dead, that his own life he took.

The suit says Tomczak said that at a conference last June,
And a tape of it was broadcast then thereafter very soon
By a Sacramento station, which played the tape right through,
And is named as codefendant, as the Harrises now sue.

Transactional Analysis is, without a doubt,
What *I'm OK—You're OK* (their book) is all about.
They're proud of their okayness, do not like to hear it said
That one of them has killed himself and therefore now is
  dead.

So now in Sacramento, in the state and federal courts,
Lawyers will be filing briefs and writing learned torts.
And preacher Larry Tomczak and station KFIA
(For saying Harris now is dead, and therefore not okay)
Must defend themselves on charges that they've slandered Dr.
  Harris.
Someone in his position it would possibly embarrass
To have it thought he'd killed himself—to act in such a way
Would certainly suggest that he was not, in fact, okay.

Now, each of us is part adult, part parent, and part child.
Sometimes we are responsible, and sometimes we are wild.
Into some sort of balance we must bring these different
  traits—
So the book they wrote, which sold so well, intelligently states.

The Harrises are both okay. He is, and she is, too.
We're all okay. I think I am. I think that you are, too.
We're all okay, one might well say, in certain ways at least,
And very likely will be till the day that we're deceased.

And part of us will bristle when we hear somebody say
That we're no longer on the scene because we've passed away.
The effect on one's self-image is bound to be quite poor
To hear such exaggeration, at the least so premature.

The case must still be argued, and we don't know who will
   win,
But we know that Thomas Harris never did do himself in.
We're all okay. You're okay, sir. You're okay, too, ma'am.
Dr. Harris is alive, you see: I sue, therefore I am.

Couple Hours Later and I Still Can't Pronounce His Name

The Chinese are inscrutable, I'm sure you've heard it said.
That word still is suitable for Chinese who are red.
And no sooner is one confident that what one thinks is true
Than suddenly they'll turn around and shift their gears on
    you.

The way that they pronounce their names is guaranteed to
    lose us.
I think they do it purposely, only to confuse us.
Just recently they changed the way that Westerners should
    spell
The names we never could pronounce, and now can't spell, as
    well.

Just take the fellow Teng Hsiao-ping, who, even as we speak,
Is visiting the U.S.A.—he's touring all this week.
His name is really Kan Tse Kao, but when he was still young
He changed the "Kao" to "Ping," the "Tse" to "Hsiao," the
    "Kan" to "Teng."

Don't ask me why he did it when only just a kid;
We only know he wanted to, and then one day he did.
Ping's a Chinese word for "peace," and Hsiao means
    "young" or "small";
He's four foot eleven, which isn't very tall.

So, according to an official source the government released,
Hsiao-ping is quite appropriate; its meaning is "small peace."
They used to spell him with a *t* (but people called him Teng).
So now they spell it with a *d* (but please don't call him
    Dang).

The *t* is pronounced just like a *d*. The *e* like *u* in "sung."
Both Tang and Dang are wrong, you see, the man is Mr.
    Dung.

Not Mr. Ping, as he was called by someone on the air.
It's first name last and last name first, that's why they put
them there.

And Hsiao began with letter *h*,
A spelling that did vex.
But that's been fixed, the *h* deep-sixed.
It's now spelled with an *x*.

And somehow in the process, Hsiao-ping became one word,
And Teng Xiaoping is two names now where once there was
a third.
And just as mystifying, causing endless mental strife,
Is what to call the woman who is with him here, his wife.

Cho Lin is what her name is (her father's name was Cho),
But she's not Madame Cho or Mrs. Cho Lin. No no no.
In Western lands she's Madame Teng, or simply called Cho
Lin.
We tried to get it right, but it seems we cannot win.

East is East and West is West—on that there's no dispute.
And that which is inscrutable is difficult to scrute.
He's only number two, they say, not Premier, but Vice.
Which proves anew of number two that two can be quite nice.

So a toast to the Vice Premier.
To his health and peace and fame.
May his dreams become still dreamier.
Yes, here's to what's-his-name.

Harry R. Truman

Once upon a time there lived an old man with a stubborn streak. Harry Truman was his name. Not Harry *S.*, but Harry *R.* Truman it was. He would sit on the porch of his lodge on the shores of Spirit Lake, and local sheriff's deputies and friends—and newspeople too—would go up to his place at the 3,200-foot level of Mount Saint Helens and they would say to him, "Harry, you'd better not stay here. You can't stay here. It's too dangerous." But Harry Truman had this stubborn streak and wasn't about to budge.

An eminent geologist once said to me, "The earth is alive, you know. It lives and breathes and moves, but our sense of time is such that we can't perceive it, except when there's an earthquake or something." The geologist said, "If you could interview a bug on a tree and you asked him, 'Is this tree alive, does it grow?' the bug would tell you, 'Of course not. I've lived here all my life and it hasn't budged an inch.'" And then the geologist said, "If you asked some old man on a mountain, 'Is this mountain alive?' he would tell you, 'No. Don't be silly, I've lived here all my life and it hasn't budged an inch.'"

I thought of that, thought of what the geologist told me when I heard the story of Harry R. Truman. For fifty-two years, Truman owned and operated the Mount Saint Helens Lodge, on the northwest slope of the mountain, up at the 3,200-foot level. Two months ago, when the sleeping mountain began to stir, the old man rode out earthquake after earthquake. He'd be knocked out of bed in the middle of the night, and finally just moved his mattress down to the basement. But when other residents of Spirit Lake were evacuated, Harry Truman simply refused to go.

"I'm not brave. I'm brave about the mountain. I couldn't understand how in the world the mountain can ever get me in Spirit Lake. I don't think it can. In any way or shape, I can't see that. But I tell you those earthquakes has got me."

Truman kept sixteen cats up there, and he made it his business to feed the local population of raccoons, too, and the pets that some of the evacuees left behind. The newspeople would go up there and snap his picture, and he'd say to them, "That mountain just doesn't dare blow up on me. I've walked this mountain for fifty years. I know her." And he would laugh. Besides, he had this secret place on high ground where he hid a grubstake and two kegs of whisky in case he got stuck up there.

This Sunday morning, Mount Saint Helens blew. The pressure of gas and magma that had caused a bulge on the north face reached the critical point. Ash, propelled from the interior, flew 63,000 feet into the air, and a shock wave leveled trees by the thousands. A pilot who flew over the area said it looked as if some giant had combed his hair. Could Harry Truman possibly have escaped? Much as everyone would like to believe he did, there doesn't seem much of a chance. Fred Johns, a fireman in Kelso, Washington, watched from thirteen miles away through a telescope as the hot ash and superheated gases roared from the crater and down the mountainside, and he saw the mud and ash roll in an avalanche, and he said to himself, if Harry Truman and his sixteen cats were alive in that lodge when the mountain erupted, they aren't now.

And now, where the lodge used to be, all there is, is steaming mud and ash. Dwight Reber, a close friend of Harry's, flew over in his helicopter and couldn't find a trace.

"There isn't a board. There's nothing," he says.

The authorities have released a list of people believed killed in the volcano eruption. On that list is one Harry R. Truman, eighty-four years old.

The Boy and the Cookie Jar

Broadcast the morning after David Frost's television interview with ex-President Richard Nixon.

Once upon a time a little boy got caught with his hand in the cookie jar. For this he knew he could get into trouble. Having been caught, he felt that he could limit or undo the damage that had been done by denying that he had been guilty of any spankable offense.

Exercising a well-known principle of juvenile behavior, he employed the technique known as "When in doubt, deny everything." And when his accuser accosted him and said, "Aha! I caught you with your hand in the cookie jar," the little boy said, "I am not a cookie snatcher."

"Well, weren't you caught in the pantry with your hand in the cookie jar, and doesn't that prove you're a cookie snatcher?"

"No," said the little boy. "That is your interpretation. But it is not my interpretation. True, there may have been times when I was in the pantry and there may have been times when, for reasons of checking on the cookie inventory, or straightening out the arrangement of the cookies within the jar, I might have reached into the jar, but what counted was my intention. And my intention was not to take out any cookies."

"But why, then, do you have that cookie in your pocket? Is that not a cookie I see hanging out?"

"You might call it a cookie hang-out," said the little boy, "but I would call it a limited, modified hang-out. The cookie in my pocket is one that I intended to carry out into the garden, where the tulips are in bloom, to feed to a little bird that I noticed there the other day, who seemed to be hungry. Now, I suppose some people might find that wicked," said the little boy. "Perhaps I was being too kind, too soft-hearted, too carried away by my love for little animals. Yes, I will plead guilty to that," he said.

"But then," said the adult, "how did those cookie crumbs get on your face?"

95

"Cookie crumbs on my face?" said the little boy. "Are there cookie crumbs on my face? Well, in that case, the crumbs must have come not from the cookies in the jar in the pantry, but from some other cookies I remember eating some time ago. The exact circumstances of those other cookies I cannot recall exactly, right at this point in time. Perhaps they were from the Girl Scout cookies that I was helping little sister to sell."

"But I thought that you had refused to help little sister."

"That is no longer operative," said the little boy, "though it may be, in some respects, at variance with the facts as heretofore stated. I did have little sister's best interests at heart. I wanted her to benefit from the experience of selling the cookies, and I tasted one only to encourage her, and let her know that the product was indeed fresh and wholesome and saleable."

"Another thing I noticed," said the adult to the little kid, "is that all the cookies were intact when they were put into the jar, but I see that there is a good-sized chunk missing out of one of them now. How did that happen?"

"I'm glad you asked me about that," said the little boy. "I, too, am mystified by the missing chunk in that cookie. In fact, that was one of the other reasons I was examining the jar. I wanted a thorough and full and complete investigation of it to see whether perhaps some kind of cookie monster was at work, or whether some other little kids . . . I'm not making any accusations, of course . . . I wouldn't accuse anyone specifically of doing it on purpose, but I thought (just possibly) some little enemy kid of mine might have botched the cookie job as a means of getting to me. I mean, they would do anything because they hate my guts, and I guess if I were in their position I would do the same thing."

"You deserve a spanking," said the adult to the little boy.

"No need," said the little boy to the adult. "I spanked myself just before you came in here."

With that, the adult gave the boy a sackful of money, which pleased the little boy to no end. Because if there was anything in this world he liked better than cookies, it was a sackful of money.

Kick Me Once and Kick Me Twice and Kick Me Once Again

There's no point in getting mad at machines, I suppose. Machines are dumb, inanimate objects, after all. Yet who among us has not, from time to time, worked up a case of frustration, resentment, and hatred over a car, a typewriter, or a soft-drink machine. People have been known to yell at machines, to hit and kick and even shoot at them. The advantage of getting mad at a machine and beating up on it is that machines (unlike people) don't harbor grudges.

At least they haven't until now.

In all these years of telling stories about weird things people do, none has struck me as more paradigmatic of our times than the story of the fellow who put a coin in a soft-drink vending machine at a gas station and the machine ate the money and produced no soft drink, and the man pulled the coin-return lever and the coin did not return and he shook and banged on the machine but no coin came back and no soft drink came out. And he kicked the vending machine on the front and then on the side, getting angrier and angrier all the time. And finally he reached in his pocket and took out a gun and pointed it at the hated machine and pulled the trigger. *Bang!* The bullet hit the machine in its vital parts, destroying it forever. It had eaten its last coin. It had failed to deliver its last soft drink. Somebody saw it all happen and turned the man in. He was arrested. Convicted. A clear case of vendicide if ever there was one.

Bad luck for him that there had been a witness, because otherwise he'd have gotten away with it. Dead machines don't tell tales. Live ones don't either, for that matter. They don't know who you are. Can't remember a thing. No way a machine can turn you in.

But wait.

Here is Robert Wenger of Monroe, Wisconsin, trying to withdraw some money from his bank account. It's Sunday, and all he wants is ten dollars, and he knows there's enough money in his account because he deposited forty dollars just the day before.

But the automatic bank teller refuses to listen to reason. Wenger then does what people often do when they get mad at machines. He hits it. Right in the face with his fist. Had the teller been a real human being, Wenger would probably not have punched him (or her) in the nose. But this wasn't a him or her. It was an it. And it was now a broken it, requiring $298 worth of repairs, as the bank people discovered when they reopened for business the next day.

By that time, of course, Wenger was long gone. but the machine turned him in. It remembered who had punched it in the nose. Wenger. Wenger, eh? Wenger, Robert L.

The computer memory said to itself, "I'm gonna get that guy if he comes in here again. In fact, even if he doesn't. Here's his name. Here's his address." It was an open-and-shut case, and Wenger was the assailant, all right.

He's been convicted of criminal damage.

So if you get mad at a machine, remember this. Machines are not as dumb as they used to be. Make sure, before you kick it, that it doesn't know where you live.

Bad Day for King Phil

It happened at a royal wedding feast. The daughter of the king himself had been married, and now there was the eating and drinking and the rejoicing that went with such an occasion. Suddenly, the flash of a knife blade. One of the king's attendants, perhaps bribed by one of his enemies, stabbed the monarch to death. The happy occasion became, in an instant, one of horror. It is in the news today, although it happened 2,314 years ago.

Someone once described being an airline pilot as "hours of boredom punctuated by moments of sheer terror." Being an archeologist is something like that: years of patient digging and cataloguing, punctuated (if one is lucky) by the pure exhilaration of discovery.

Professor Manolis Andronikos of the University of Thessaloniki, Greece, has been digging around the farming village of Vergina for the last forty years, looking for Macedonian tombs. Macedonia was an ancient kingdom that came to be one of the great powers of the world in its time.

The professor had made some finds, but pursued his task methodically, taking each thing in its turn, waiting until one area had been thoroughly excavated before moving on to the next. As long ago as the early 1950s, he had noticed something that was particularly interesting, he thought—a forty-foot-high mound about a hundred yards wide. To the professor it looked man-made, and he suspected it might contain an unusually large tomb—perhaps even one of royalty. But the excavation there did not begin until very recently—this past August 30.

A bulldozer uncovered first the remains of a funeral pyre, with metal harness fittings for three or four horses. Andronikos knew that meant the person buried below must be of high rank, whoever he was. Next they found a marble doorway topped with a wonderful fresco. It showed mounted hunters pursuing game through a forest. And surrounding that fresco was a white facade highlighted in bright blue and red. "We knew at once," said Andronikos, "that no common mortal was buried in such a tomb."

Seventeen feet below the surface they found two rooms, which they entered by breaking a hole in the back. Inside the larger of the two chambers they found a suit of royal armor—a gold-trimmed breastplate, a helmet and shin guards, a shield of leather and wood. And nearby, a golden diadem—a thin crown, just like the ones carved on the statues of Macedonian kings.

In a marble sarcophagus was a golden casket, its lid embossed with the sunburst symbol of Macedonian monarchs. Andronikos says the bones inside the casket were covered with a wreath of gold leaves. He took his flashlight and crawled around the chamber on his hands and knees, and he found what he now calls his "proof of proofs"—five tiny statuette heads. He took them home with him that night, put them in a row at the foot of his bed, and stared at them all night. "No question," he says. One was the face of the king stabbed to death at the wedding of his daughter, Philip II of Macedonia.

Two other statuette heads were of Philip's parents. Another was of his wife. And the fifth head was the most familiar of all. It's why archeologists today are saying Andronikos' find is the most important in Greece for decades. For the son of Philip II of Macedonia, represented in that fifth statuette head, became, after his father's murder, not only a powerful king whose army was feared from Athens to India, but in his time the ruler of most of the known world.

History calls him Alexander the Great.

So it is that under 26,160 cubic yards of dirt in a Greek farming village, there is in this morning's news the reminder of a murder committed in 336 B.C.

Of government there is no lack;
The government is on your back.
Although we need it, I suppose,
We're paying for it through the nose.

The Government

A Carpet on the Floor Means a Boondoggle at the Door

Do you know what government bureaucrats sit at? They sit at desks, of course. Therefore, the federal government owns many, many desks. Do you know what bureaucrats sit on? They sit on chairs, of course. And therefore, the federal government owns many, many chairs. Do you know how many desks and chairs and filing cabinets and the like the federal government has stored? Well, I'm not surprised that you don't know that, because the federal government doesn't know it either.

The federal government owns a lot of things that you and I wouldn't have much use for personally—missiles and tanks and battleships and hydroelectric dams and monuments and government buildings, of course. The federal government owns more than half a million government buildings in and out of Washington. In those buildings, it has workers who use quite common, ordinary stuff that you and I might not be totally unfamiliar with—chairs and tables and desks and typewriters and file cabinets and so on. The bigger the government gets, the more committees and departments and agencies there are, the more stuff is needed for them to sit at and sit on and write regulations with and so forth. Back fifty years ago, when over half the government employees were mailmen, the government didn't need so much stuff, since mailmen weren't supposed to do much sitting around anyway. As far as I know, mailmen still don't have desks to sit at. Their bosses do, of course, but whatever its failings, the Postal Service is possibly the only government-sponsored activity where there are still more people standing up than there are sitting down.

I remember a few years ago our friend Andy Rooney tried to find out what made Washington tick, and he discovered that there were, in the official General Services Administration catalogue, several different kinds of chairs, ranging from big, important-looking chairs to unimposing, ordinary little chairs that would not impress anybody. Rooney pointed out at the time that there were sixteen different kinds of chairs for government employees, and eighteen different grades of government employee. He figured that meant there was one type of chair for each grade, with the bottom two grades having to stand.

Nowadays, though, the government has been improved and streamlined many times. There are more agencies, departments, bureaus, and committees than ever. And you can't very well have a chairperson without a chair, can you? Nor can you table a motion without a table, or regulate things without regulations. So there are all these file cabinets and other pieces of furniture.

In October, Senator Lawton Chiles of Florida toured one of seventy-eight government warehouses where useable furniture is stored in the Washington area. Some of the stuff needed repair, but some of it was brand new, still wrapped in plastic and in the original cartons. Yet, despite these seventy-eight warehouses full of stuff, federal agencies spent 1.2 billion dollars on new furniture in the 1970s. There's some reason to suspect that some government agencies don't have the foggiest idea what they have, and go out and buy things they've already got. Some agencies do keep inventories, and the General Accounting Office says it figures we've got 6.8 million dollars in furniture stashed away in over a hundred different storage sites.

Congressional hearings on government furniture, and how much of it there is and how little we know about how much there is, start today.

Sometimes You Can Do Just as Well, Telling Uncle to Go to Hell

Out in California, there's a city, El Cajon,
Which, like so many cities, finds expenditures have grown.
And it's had to raise its taxes over what they once had been,
Because in El Cajon more is going out than coming in.
That's a common situation, as anyone can tell,
Which many individuals are coping with as well.
So, when there is a chance to help defray some civic cost,
They seize it lest the happy opportunity be lost.

When you are a bureaucrat, there's very little thanks
For making up the many forms, for filling in the blanks
That contain the needed data for the agencies to file,
Or stack upon each other in a neat and dandy pile.
But you have to have the paperwork to keep the process
    going.
To feed the need for rules to heed, the paperwork keeps
    flowing.

The story that we tell today by no means stands alone;
It has to do with something that occurred in El Cajon.
It could have happened anywhere, that we have to warn you,
Although in this instance it occurred in California.
El Cajon's a city, an officer of which
Is the Personnel Administrator, fellow name of Fitch.

John Fitch could see no reason, and could perceive no harm,
In allowing Uncle Sam to pay for burglar alarms.
Money from the government, absolutely free,
Derived, of course, from taxpayers like him and you and me.
A program that's administered all throughout the nation
By the Federal Law Enforcement Assistance Administration.

El Cajon was eligible, so the lawyer stated.
On the basis of its size and needs, the city rated

Money back for money spent already out of hand.
Eight thousand dollars' worth. The city sure could use eight
　　grand.
Such was the logic at the time, such was the thinking which
Led the Personnel Department and its officer, John Fitch,
To start the wheels to turning so that Washington would send
The money back to El Cajon, on other things to spend.

Sounds simple, I am sure, and so it sounded then to Fitch.
Eight thousand bucks is not enough to make the city rich.
But it would help to put some coins into the city's purse
If what they'd spent on those alarms Uncle Sam would
　　reimburse.
So Fitch sent a note of inquiry, thus touching off the storms—
The lightning and the thunder and the heavy rain of forms.

There were forms enough to curl your hair and cause your
　　teeth to ache.
Forms for the equipment, and each model, year, and make.
Forms about the city in the smallest detail known
About the population and the thieves of El Cajon.
Forms to show compliance with a thousand laws and rules,
About the cops of El Cajon, the firemen, the schools.
Forms that dealt with civil rights and equal opportunity,
With blanks that could not be ignored, at least not with
　　impunity.

When Fitch saw what he'd have to do to get the town the
　　money,
He was not in the least amused—he did not find it funny.
In the labor it would take to get the paperwork completed
The cost involved would be so great the purpose was defeated.
What use in getting such a grant, John Fitch sadly said,
If the money we get back we're spending getting it instead?

Why go to all the bother and the labor costs and such,
If to get the funds from Washington costs every bit as much?

Free money from the government sounds very, very nice,
But El Cajon has learned that, though it's free, it has its
    price.
Two hundred man-hours it would cost, should they decide to
    let it,
So Fitch wrote back to Washington and told them to forget it.
The forms remain unfilled, and nothing's written in the
    blanks,
And El Cajon has, in effect, said thank you, but no thanks!

None of the Above

In Louisiana, they contemplate
A primary election in that old state.
And among the candidates for Gov.
Is one named None of the Above.

Though some may think it's a crying shame,
That happens to be the fellow's name.
He's run before without much success,
But figures this should be his year. Yes,
Because None of the Above, unless he's wrong,
Is who the voters wanted all along.

In Louisiana, one Luther Knox
Is a candidate who's a sly old fox.
He wants to be governor, nothing more,
And though he's run for other jobs before,
He's not a politician; doesn't have the knack—
"I'm what you might call a lumberjack."

So the thing in which Knox has been very good
Is felling trees and sawing wood.
But he qualified to be a candidate,
And he is, as all the records duly state.
He's due to be listed in the ballot box.
"I had qualified as L. D. Knox."

But here is the thing that made him blue in the face:
"We have six major candidates in the race."
But they called Knox "minor," did the major six,
And their wagons he really wanted to fix.

So he thought up a way to do more than elect.
A name change!
"Which gives you the right to reject . . ."
If you don't like the other candidates for Gov.
"That's my name now. I'm None of the Above."

None of the Above worked hard to get in this position.
"I went through the courts, filed a petition."
So L. D. Knox exists no more. And he has no remorse.
"And signed it, and then the judge had to sign it, of course."

And so the ballot must be changed to so accommodate.
"Of course, I've applied to the secretary of state."
And what did the secretary of the state then do?
He's Paul Hardy, and he's running for governor, too.
And Above's petition made him frown.
"The secretary of state turned me down."

None of the Above thinks they should have smiled, but
"They have refused, and petitions have been filed,"
So the courts may give the case a little shove
In the matter of the candidate named None of the Above.
And the major six are clucking. They're in something of a
    stew—
"And that's what I was, of course, trying to do."

The reason the officials give for not being receptive
Is that "none of the above" can't be a name. It's too deceptive.
But Mr. Above is sure the courts will want it solved,
"Because it is a constitutional question involved."

And please, he says, don't call me that. I'll give you other
    ways.
"If you call me Mr. Above, then it changes the meaning of
    the phrase."
For it's not Above he wants to be, but None of the Above—
A name that he thinks anyone is surely bound to love.
His eleven kids are Knoxes still. His wife won't join the game
    yet
As Mrs. None of the Above.
"She hasn't changed her name yet."

But None of the Above is now campaigning for support.
But it won't fit on a button, so,
"I call myself NOTA for short."

Cost of Not Running

It costs a lot of money to run for office these days. That's no surprise. What is surprising is that it costs money even *not* to run for office.

Joe Waggonner, Democrat of Louisiana, has been a member of the House of Representatives for a long time now—nine terms. And earlier this year he decided that enough is enough, and he let it be known that he would not be running for a tenth term.

Being in the Congress of the United States is by no means the very worst job in the world, however, and no sooner did Waggonner say that he would not be occupying that particular seat any more than several people came along to say that they would very much like to. There are, as a matter of fact, nine candidates for the Fourth District seat representing northwest Louisiana. There's a primary election coming up on the sixteenth of this month, and then the general election will be on the seventh of November.

It is required by law that the candidates file reports with the Louisiana secretary of state, spelling out how much money they have raised and how much they have spent on their various campaigns. This week the secretary of state's office received a report from the Joe D. Waggonner Committee of Shreveport, which has some $67,174 in the bank. The candidates seeking Waggonner's job are expected to spend on the order of a million dollars trying to get it. That is an average of about $110,000 apiece for the nine hopefuls.

But here is what caught our eye. In the reporting period from the first of July through the first of September, 1978, the Joe D. Waggonner Committee of Shreveport spent one dollar and forty cents. Not very much, but offhand it would seem a lot of money to spend to not run for Congress.

I mean, surely one can find some pity
For the Joe D. Waggonner Committee.

It can't really be any fun
When the man you're boosting does not run.
When the congressman you feel is fine
Decides to make term number nine
The last one that he ever will
Spend in that seat up on Capitol Hill.

Your fondest hope it tends to dash
When he for whom you have raised some cash
Elects to do what you'd not suspected,
And does not attempt to be reelected.
But who would think and who'd believe
That the Waggonner group from the port of Shreve
Would have to spend a certain sum—
Regardless of where it's coming from—

To pay the cost, however small,
Of not soliciting votes at all.
It must make Joe D. Waggonner laugh
To think that somehow on his behalf
Was spent a figure rather sporty.
Campaign expenses: a dollar forty.

Just where the dollar forty went,
Exactly on what the committee spent
The money, is something we do not know.
The figures are simply there to show
That in times when costs tend to be immense
The sum of a dollar and forty cents
Was spent, the accountant's numbers state,
For a man who isn't a candidate.

Now, we all can see (there's no need to mention)
That a politician, to get attention,
Must spend a little dough-re-mi
So his stands on issues will duly be
Made known to the voters, so that they
Will vote for him on election day.

To win elections, one quickly learns,
One has to spend for the votes he earns.
What may surprise you a little bit
Is to have to spend even when you quit.
A man who's running who wants to be
A Congressman down in old D.C.
Must pay for his ads and his campaign spot.
But it turns out even if he is not,

Campaign expenses will not have ceased.
It's going to cost that man at least
A dollar forty (one-four-oh),
Though where it will go we do not know.

In the years he spent up on the Hill
Joe Waggonner's voted on many a bill.
He's seen expenditures rise and rise
To an astronomical sort of size.
As he leaves the Congress he will not weep.
At a dollar forty, he gets off cheap.

Sunshine Act

There's only so much daylight in each day,
Yet we make it lighter later when we say,
To make the daylight hours seem like more,
"It's five o'clock," when it is only four.

And thus in summer do we kid ourselves
In order for a while to rid ourselves
Of what will come despite us all.
No matter, night will surely fall.

We say that it is eight when it is seven,
We say that it is twelve when it's eleven—
Which people seem to think gives them more fun.
More time to romp and revel in the sun.

And Congress in its wisdom and its power
Has standardized the daylight-saving hour
To deal with local laws in great profusion
(Which has led to some remarkable confusion).

You'd have daylight-saving in some little town,
Where the place across the street had turned it down.
And it became a little hard to say,
In certain cases, what's the time of day.

That's why down in Washington they saw
They had to have a daylight-saving law
So that from the spring right on through the fall
What went for one would also go for all.

But now, I am afraid, I have to warn you
That out there in the state of California
They've come up with an idea that is new:
Not one hour's daylight-saving time, but two.

Bob Wilson says his so-called Sunshine Act
Is based upon the weight of solid fact,
That making this adjustment in the time
Would bring about a lower rate of crime.

And, being very sharp and realistic,
He points out the appropriate statistic
That more cars tend to crash when it is night.
And if that traffic-safety log is right

It seems the only proper thing to do
Is, when it's four o'clock, say that it's two.
And Wilson says this little self-duplicity
Will mean a lessened use of electricity.

For if this law is passed, he says, why, then
We won't need any lights until it's ten.
And what makes that particularly nice is
It's bound to help relieve the power crisis.

It's something that can easily be fixed,
Although the blessing may not be unmixed.
For something will assuredly be said
About the problems getting kids to bed.

And what might bother farmers like the dickens
Is how to train their pigs and cows and chickens.
But what is that, compared to the felicity
Of having fun, and saving electricity?

And if we can with two hours so contrive,
Then why not three or four, or even five?
If we play our cards right, from now until the fall
We may not see the sun go down at all.

We all will be in bed when it is noon,
Asleep beneath the summer midday moon.

And think what we'll get done when it is night
When the sun beats down with all that heat and light.

And why, I ask you now, should we stop there
When surely some assemblyman with flair
Will come to realize (he will do it one day)
That people aren't crazy about Monday. . . .

He'll take the daylight law, improve and polish it,
And Monday will be gone. He'll just abolish it.
Put Tuesday where the Monday used to be.
The principle is simple, don't you see?

And are there not some good and valid reasons
For eliminating certain months and seasons?
Soon there will be no one to remember
When it was late at night or late December.

And we will all be happy, having fun,
And laugh and play beneath the midnight sun.

Rhinoceros

Stranger than fiction is that which is true,
And I'll prove that again here before I am through.
And the tale that we tell this particular morn
Has to do with a certain rhinoceros horn.
It turned out that wasn't really the truth,
For in fact it was one hippopotamus tooth.
And the fact that those things have a similar look
Took President Carter off of the hook.

In a *Wall Street Journal* story on Wednesday of this week
Was a reference to the incident about which now we speak.
In a piece about Brzezinski, also known as Mr. Zbig,
Were several little anecdotes. Reporters like to dig.
And one of those referred to something earlier this year,
When Mobuto Sese Seko paid a visit from Zaire.

Mobuto is the president and he found himself one day
Visiting the President of the U.S.A.
And the *Journal* said he brought along a certain little gift,
Which, when they read about it, made the Wildlife Fund
    quite miffed.
For what Mobuto brought along to give to Jimmy C.
Was the horn of a rhinoceros, or so it seemed to be.

And Brzezinski wrote the President a note to the effect
That rhino horns were famous for what you might not
    suspect.
The note from Mr. Zbig, the *Wall Street Journal* story stated,
Said that as aphrodisiacs such horns were highly rated.
It went on to ask the President, the *Journal* piece did say,
If he'd be so kind as please to let him borrow it someday.

The President wrote back and said he'd do that friendly deed,
If Brzezinski really wanted it, and would certify his need.

And Mr. Carter added that he'd also need to see
Who, if Zbig did borrow it, his partner would be.
The story ran on Wednesday, as we've already said,
And it raised some angry eyebrows as soon as it was read,

For rhinos are endangered. They are listed on the list.
And a gift of such a rhino horn could not just be dismissed.
The World Wildlife Fund protested that such a souvenir
Should not have been accepted from the leader of Zaire.
Mr. Carter hadn't realized that there'd be such a flap
Over what Mr. Mobuto had dumped there in his lap.

But yesterday, the White House said, there'd been a big
    mistake.
The gift was not a rhino horn, nor was it just a fake.
What it was, they now all realize, for now they are much
    wiser,
Was a tooth of hippopotamus, a lower-right incisor.
And the hippo's not endangered; there are lots of them
    around.
At least, there in Zaire, a lot of hippos can be found.

A rhino and a hippo are not at all the same,
Though each has size and also quite unspellable a name.
So the President is off the hook, now that we know the truth,
That the rhino horn is not a horn, but just a hippo tooth.
The Wildlife Fund is mollified, that group that wrote the
    letter.
They say, since it's a hippo tooth, they feel a whole lot better.

But that Mr. Zbig confused that tooth with horn of a
    rhinoceros
They find a bit amusing and perhaps a bit preposterous.
Both animals, it's true, are fond of wallowing in mud,
But as human aphrodisiacs, a hippo tooth's a dud.
And here we have the bottom line, for that is where the
    bottom is:
A rhino horn's as useless as the tooth of hippopotamus.

117

Fraud, Etc.

There is no more "fraud, abuse, and waste" in the Department of Health, Education and Welfare.* Secretary Patricia Harris has seen to that. At a recent meeting of her executive staff, Mrs. Harris eliminated "fraud, waste, and abuse" at HEW by the simple expedient of ordering the phrase "fraud, waste, and abuse" be eliminated and replaced throughout the department with the words "program misuse and management inefficiency."

A recent Inspector General's report found a lot of waste at HEW, not to mention fraud and abuse. So it's rather interesting to note that from now on there won't be any fraud, abuse, or waste at all—only a little program misuse and management inefficiency. Now, if you had to choose between "fraud, abuse, and waste" and "program misuse and management inefficiency," I suppose "program misuse and management inefficiency" are better, since the words are far longer, fuzzier, less pejorative, and more pretentious, and therefore far more pleasing to bureaucratic ears.

Sure enough, at least one senior executive at HEW, Herbert Doggette of the Social Security Administration, got up from that meeting with Secretary Patricia Harris, and followed right up on her order to replace the phrase "fraud, abuse, and waste" with the phrase "program misuse and management inefficiency." He shot off a memo to his own people saying he agreed "that the Secretary's terminology reflects what we are measuring and working to eliminate. The change is effective immediately. Please see that it is effected in your areas of responsibility."

And so, at HEW, with the merciful mandate of a memorandum, no more "fraud, abuse, and waste."

If fraud and abuse and waste are what trouble you,
You'll approve what they've done at the old HEW.
They've wiped out "abuse, fraud, and waste," and the like
With the stroke of a pen, with a surgical strike.

Now "waste" has been wasted, "abuse" got the noose,
And no longer is "fraud" still abroad on the loose.
Mrs. Harris has made her patrician decision
And has wiped out those things with amazing precision.

"Fraud, waste, and abuse" will no longer embarrass
The team that reports to Patricia R. Harris.
"Fraud, waste, and abuse" simply do not exist.
They are gone—and good riddance! They'll never be missed.
And the only things left to cause trouble or care
Are a little "program misuse and management inefficiency"
    here and there.

All us citizen taxpayers have to applaud
This daring attack on abuse, waste, and fraud.
HEW now is officially free
Of fraud, of abuse, and of waste—of all three.
It's devoid now of fraud and of waste and abuse.
We are much better off with some "program misuse."

"Fraud" is an ugly word. "Waste" seems so crude.
"Abuse" is offensive and borders on rude.
And such words in a grand departmental report
Are insufficiently polysyllabic, too short.

"Program misuse" and "management inefficiency"
Do not suffer from this very deadly deficiency.
They're lawyerlike, long-lasting, lingering names,
Intended to bore one, but not to inflame.
You'll be happy to know, since the bill you must foot,
That from now on "abuse, waste, and fraud" are kaput.

*And now there isn't any HEW either.

Congress

"Whan that Aprille with his shoures soote
The droghte of March hath perced to the roote,"
Then longen folk in Congress of U.S.
To go on pilgrimage while in recess.

Thither do they go and also yon.
The Capitol is empty, for they're gone.
A goodly group are they and also merry,
Who, at the time of blooming of the cherry,
Do feel the urge to leave their stately dome
To go into the world and that to roam

In numbers one might smile to contemplate.
Not one or two, but a whole one hundred eight.
The Speaker of the House, yclept O'Neill,
Most certainly this wanderlust did feel,

And with a group that numbered seventeen
Did off to Ireland, land of shamrock green,
From which his forebears set out long ago.
The Irish love to travel, you may know.

And they'll stop awhile in England
And in Hungary to find some facts.
Such dedicated people, it is clear,
To be in England, now that April's here.

While that group's led by the good Speaker, Tip,
John Brademus, the Democratic whip,
Is leading eighteen colleagues on a visit
To Russia. Now, that's not a junket, is it?

And who of us would dare to doubt the right
Of Democratic leader (that's Jim Wright)

To lead a pilgrimage to mainland China?
His motives, one is sure, could not be finer.

They'll see exotic things while they are there:
The many mysteries of China fair.
And possibly, while they are at the wall,
They will run into a group familiar all.

That's something that might very well be done,
For another Congress group of twenty-one
Will be visiting the Forbidden City.
They're from the Armed Services Committee.

And the Senate won't be left out in the lurch.
Five committee members, led by Church,
Are visiting in China now as well.
Yes, China is quite "in" (as one can tell).

Three different delegations, now you see.
That many out of Congress! Forty-three . . .
A number that I do believe is more
Than one often finds on House and Senate floor.

But a Baker man there was who stayed at home;
This time he found it difficult to roam.
The Air Force chose his plane to take away,
When some speech on peanut warehouse he did say.

There are other Congressmen in Paris at this time
And other cities where there's pleasant clime:
Berlin and Brussels, Cairo, Tokyo,
Geneva, Prague, and Dublin do they go.

Not junketing, but needed trips, to know.
Full wise is he that can himselfen know.
So, know ye all, your Congressmen come through.
They said they'd go to great lengths, and they do.

Carter's Rabbit

It's always open season on the President, it seems.
No matter what he does, there's always somebody who
    screams.
He's attacked by the Republicans and threatened from within.
A President has got to have a thick and rugged skin.
He's attacked by critics in the press, both from the left and
    right.
With business and with unions he must be prepared to fight.

He must struggle with our enemies and even with our friends.
The heat must be just terrible. The fighting never ends.
With all the special interests and with citizens irate,
Of every stripe and point of view, it must be too great.
Not to know who will attack you next must be a little rough.
But, as if there weren't enemies and predators enough
To make a man defensive and pugnacious just by habit,
Mr. Carter now has been attacked by an offensive rabbit.

It happened back in April, but it's only now come out,
But the slight delay in telling you should not inspire doubt.
For we have it on authority that one day, down in Plains
(He was down there on vacation, our authority explains),
While the President was fishing in a certain fishing hole,
Just minding his own business, alone with fishing pole . . .

Mr. Carter fished away, alone in his canoe
Doing what a lot of us might wish that we could do.
As completely unaggressive as anyone could wish,
Not threatening at all (unless, of course, you are a fish).

When suddenly, the story goes, there was a nearby splash,
And out there in the water, swimming toward him like a
    flash . . .
Hissing, so the story goes, as if it were a snake,
Flashing, gnashing teeth—as ugly a face as it could make—

Was a rabbit. Yes, a rabbit, with his bunny nostrils flared.
Coming at the Presidential boat, his eyes with anger glared.

Mr. Carter did not flinch, we're told, but grabbed a paddle
    quick,
And flailed out at the rabbit, with the paddle as a stick.
It was just a brief encounter and it didn't then seem funny—
The President attacked that way. And by a killer bunny!

But by dint of speedy reflexes, and paddle from canoe,
Driving off the perpetrator. Where he went, though, no one
    knew.
At first, when Mr. Carter told his story of the bunny,
His friends did not believe him. They would just look at him
    funny.
And we hear that Mr. Carter was just the least bit stung
Not to be believed, when he, with Presidential tongue
Told of the adventure he experienced out there.
Did folks doubt Teddy Roosevelt when he talked about bear?

But it seems that Mr. Carter could prove that it was true.
The White House had some photographs, and what he had
    them do
Was enlarge a certain picture, and sure enough, my dears,
The creature had a cottontail and fuzzy rabbit ears.
But they won't release the picture, whatever be their goal,
For that would be to give away his favorite fishing hole.

There's got to be, it seems to me, another sort of reason,
And perhaps it would be logical, connected to the season.
For Easter was in April, when all of this took place,
And perhaps the White House feared there'd be an awful loss
    of face
If the President were seen attacking not just any beast
But a little bunny rabbit right around the Easter feast.
For it would not be good politics, nor thought about as funny
If people thought the President attacked the Easter Bunny.

123

"When the going gets tough, the tough get going"—
I wish I knew what that meant.
I was told long ago to have get-up-and-go.
And that's when I got up and went.

Business

Who Owns What

It used to be that you could tell
What a company had to sell.
By simply seeing what its name was,
You would figure out just what its game was.
Car companies all made cars.
Cigar companies turned out cigars.
And corporations that made soap
Would not make cake or coffee. Nope.

But in the business world today
They would. And very likely may.
From names today you can't begin
To figure out what line they're in.

Okay, folks, here we go.
Some facts that some of you may know
On who does what and who owns whom.
Stand back now, and give me room!

Campbell's soup, the old soup classic,
Also makes a pickle, Vlasic.
Chesebrough-Pond's makes Pond's cold cream,
Ragú spaghetti sauce, and Vaseline.
Colgate-Palmolive gets your thanks
For Hebrew National salami and franks.
The same outfit that makes Sara Lee
Makes Fuller brushes, too, you see.

Did you know that Butter Ball turkey was
Produced by the firm that makes Playtex bras?
Or that No-Nonsense of the pantyhose
Makes nonsense—TV's "Laverne & Shirley" shows?
If you ride a bus on a trip you're takin',
You're involved with a firm that brings home the bacon.

You may not know it, but you are,
'Cause the Greyhound Corporation owns Armour Star.

ITT makes Wonder Bread,
And a lot of other things, it's said.
If you've ever stayed at a Sheraton Hotel,
You've been ITT's guest there, as well.
Mattel makes Barbie dolls. That you knew.
But do you know what else they do?
They have herds of elephants, does Mattel.
'Cause they own the Ringling Brothers Circus as well.

The Liggett Group makes L&M,
And Alpo dog food is owned by them.
Miles Laboratories are the lads
That make Alka-Seltzer and SOS scouring pads.
And cookies aren't the only business Nabisco is in;
They make Rose Milk products for your skin.
You get businesses quite unrelated
When outfits get conglomerated.

Norton Simon, Inc., makes Halston's stuff,
And Max Factor cosmetics, but that's not enough:
Hunt's tomato products are Simon-sent.
As are Avis cars that you can rent,
And Scotch and soda—I'll tell you why,
They own both Johnny Walker and Canada Dry.

Pepsi-Cola makes well-known drinks,
And Wilson sporting goods from courts to links.
Sports equipment for the games you play,
And snacks that they market as Frito-Lay.

Procter & Gamble makes Cheer and Tide,
And some other things that they don't hide;
Duncan Hines cake mixes are included in these,
And Charmin toilet paper (please don't squeeze).

Quaker Oats makes oatmeal and Ken-L Ration feed,
And Fisher-Price toys when it's toys you need.

Winstons aren't R. J. Reynolds' only thing.
They also sell chow mein; you know it as Chun King.
Unilever makes Aim (that's a toothpaste, see),
And owns Thomas J. Lipton, which is known for tea.

Well, I shouldn't really be a bit surprised, I guess,
Since Holt, Rinehart and Winston is owned by CBS.

Laundromat

From a small Louisiana town, a man named Brian King
To the high court of the U.S.A. a certain case did bring.
King operates a laundromat, and sometimes, he believes,
The courts could use some cleaning up in how they deal with
    thieves.

One night he took some pictures of a thief inside his store,
And he posted them for all the world to see them,
    furthermore.
The thief was pictured big as life, with hands right in the till.
He pleaded guilty to the crime, no doubt of that, but still
King put those pictures up. Much to his disbelief,
The judge then fined him five times more than he had fined
    the thief.

In nineteen hundred seventy-three, on an October night,
Brian King, a laundry owner, set his lens just right
To capture with his camera the act of an intruder.
If taking such a picture's rude, why, breaking in is ruder.

And King had really had it with break-ins at his store.
He'd been hit there at the laundromat too many times before.
And sure enough, the camera, that very night, in fact,
Caught somebody in the place, and snapped him in the act.

Teenager Michael Norris had broken through the locks
And was pilfering the money from the soda-vending box,
No question who it was at all who broke into the place,
For right there on the film was Michael Norris and his face.

With the help of King's two photographs, a "guilty" plea was
    sought,
And Norris pleaded guilty, seeing how he had been caught.

The judge fined him a hundred bucks, and that, he felt, had ended it.
Although he sentenced him to jail, he right away suspended it.

Now, King still had the photographs and thought as a deterrent,
He'd put them in the laundry, though decorative they weren't.
"Caught in the Act!" the caption said beneath the pictures two,
And "Michael has a record now," and that, of course, was true.

But King was hauled into the court. He found that quite absurd.
And sitting on the bench was State Judge Martin Laird the Third.
Now, Michael Norris had complained that up in public sight
Were the pictures King had taken of the burglary that night.

And Judge Laird laid down the law to King with a judicial frown,
And ordered him without delay to take those pictures down.
To have those pictures in his place there on the laundry wall,
Had violated Michael's rights, his privacy and all.

And that was not the only thing, was not the final word
Then spoken by his honor, State Judge Martin Laird the Third.
Since Mr. King this awful thing had done, the judge did say,
Five hundred dollars damages to Norris, King must pay.

So Norris, if the case held up, just as His Honor said,
Despite his hundred-dollar fine, was four hundred ahead.
The case moved slowly upward through the ladder of appeal.
The judges read the record of the case, how both the parties feel,

And decided King was trying, with the picture-posting tack,
To force the pictured burglar to give the money back.
And that King had no right to do, the appeals courts duly
found;
To the U.S. high court the case seemed truly bound.

The Supreme Court of the U.S.A. was asked to hear the case
That grew out of those pictures King had made of Norris'
face.
But yesterday, in passing, the high court of the land
Refused to enter in the case and let the judgment stand.

Perhaps they'll reconsider it on some new and other grounds
Than King and his attorneys up to now have found.
But King's lawyer says he did his best and tried to make a
case of it.
He thought that in those pictures was injustice on the face of
it.

So if you should see a burglar in your place one of these
nights,
For goodness' sake, be careful you don't violate his rights.
Brian King, the laundry owner, wiser now, if meaner,
Believes he knows what people mean by "taken to the
cleaner."

Turkey vs. Hog

In a case in U.S. District Court,
According to a news report,
The hog producers of the U.S.A.
Are bringing suit because, they say,
The turkey industry now uses
A word that misleads and confuses.

There's something called a "turkey ham"
Which pork producers call a sham.
The turkey people don't see why
They cannot call a turkey thigh
A turkey ham, and so they do.
So now the hog producers sue.

And someone with a judge's robe
Will hear the case, will weigh and probe.
And lawyers' briefs that are immense,
From both the plaintiff and defense,
Will argue, in lawyers' words,
The subtleties of hams and birds.

A turkey, as you all well know,
Cannot fly, and runs quite slow.
The reason that he cannot fly:
He's small of wing and large of thigh.
And though, as birds go, he is big,
You'd not confuse him with a pig.

The pig does not have wings at all.
He makes the turkey look quite small.
He's totally devoid of feathers.
His skin is used for certain leathers.
The turkey doesn't have a snout.
And what this case is all about,

The one in Norfolk's District Court
That's mentioned in the news report,
Is a product, in the butcher's case.
That turns a hog producer's face
Purple with his indignation:
Turkey ham. That designation

Used for turkey, fine meat, cured,
Not ham at all, please be assured.
But regulations of the day,
Put out by the USDA,
Define a turkey ham as legal,
Not made of pig or duck or eagle,

But turkey thigh, cured some way
That makes it taste like ham, some say.
The companies that sell real pork
From California to New York,
From Texas all the way to Maine,
Say this is nonsense. They complain

That turkey's turkey, ham is ham—
The only kind of ham what am!
They want the court to now insist
That turkey packers must desist
From using ham in any name,
Since pigs and birds are not the same.

The hog producers say to use
"Turkey ham" tries to confuse
The public into thinking that
There is some creature winged and fat,
With feathers and a curly tail,
Who snorts into his feeding pail.

Who struts along, as turkeys will,
But oinks a lot and dines on swill.

And lays big eggs, sometimes a dud,
And likes to wallow in the mud.
The turkey people simply say:
Why, not at all! And in no way

Is ham a word that just applies
To pigs and to their porcine thighs.
They claim no one concerned with swine
Can say that "this word 'ham' is mine!"
No way, they say, and most effusive,
Is ham a special pig exclusive.

The case may run a good long time.
The issues are complex and prime.
With witnesses for either side,
As business interests will collide.
No doubt about it, it's a biggy.
I wonder if they'll call Miss Piggy.

Beer

Germans, you'll not be shocked to hear,
Are rather fond of drinking beer.
They drink it down both day and night.
They drink it dark, they drink it light.

They drink a beer to quench their thirsts.
They drink beer to wash down their wursts.
They drink beer slow to make it last
Or pour it down their gullets fast.

And what they love the very best
Is Munich at Oktoberfest.
To Germans, it's unthinkable
To make their beer undrinkable.

Governments try to take good care o' ya,
And that is why in old Bavaria
In the Year of Our Lord 1516,
A certain problem was foreseen.

A kindly duke named Wilhelm Second,
One day very wisely reckoned
That the thing his people held most dear
Was a good Bavarian stein of beer.

We need a law, he began to think,
That will standardize this beer we drink,
To define without the slightest doubt
What German beer is all about.

To make a beer that is flawless
Malt, hops, and water. *Das ist alles.*
This alone is the legal brew,
And he signed the document, Wilhelm Two.

The centuries have come and gone,
But German beer has continued on.
From the sixteenth century to the twentieth
The Germans brewed their beer—plentieth—

Abiding by Duke Wilhelm's law,
Even though, as he foresaw,
Other people in other places
Would turn out absolute disgraces.

And when someone asked them, "What is this here?"
They'd claim it was a glass of beer,
When what they poured into their glasses
Really tasted like molasses.

Not water, malt, or finest hops,
But rather more like soda pops.
Now, all of this is just by way
Of bringing you up to today.

For this week there appeared in Bonn
A fellow who's an expert on
(Or so it's indicated here)
The subject of (of all things) beer.

Looking like somebody's uncle
Came one Professor Dieter Runckel
Before the German Bundestag
To drop his bomb like thunderstag.

What Professor Runckel had to say
Was that it would surely pay
If everyone in EBC
Would only sit down and agree

To change the laws that limit beer
To just those three components there.

Now, what we mean by the EBC
Is the Common Market, don't you see?

Which is working out a plan for Europe
Where beer could taste like maple syrup.
Under which, if it goes through,
Certain additives would do.

Such as, say, ascorbic acid.
How can anyone stay placid
When with glucose beer is padded,
Protiolytic enzyme added.

Sulfur dioxide would be okay
If the Common Market had its way.
All those countries do allow
That stuff in the beer they're selling now.

And we Americans also think
Such stuff belongs in the beer we drink.
But not the Germans. So far, *nein*.
They'll suffer nothing in their stein

But what was laid out by and by
By that old Duke Wilhelm I-and-I.
The lawmakers told the professor
They would not let their beer be lesser.

A German drinker I never knew who
Wanted beer to taste like Yoo Hoo.
They threw old Dieter Runckel out
And left not even the slightest doubt

For anyone with ears to hear
The way they feel about their beer.
Ein prosit! Ein prosit! And Dieter Runckel, scat!
The world safe for *gemütlichkeit*! Okay, I'll drink to that.

"Only when a tree has fallen can you take the measure of it. It is the same with a man."

—Anne Morrow Lindberg

Obits

Hitchcock

Real art always reaches into the subconscious, touching the part of us that dreams. Alfred Hitchcock was an artist, and the dreams he touched were our nightmares.

Fear is part of the human condition in the age of anxiety, and there are things to be afraid of. We know that. That is why Alfred Hitchcock did not think of his movies as mysteries.

"Because, you see, mystery is withholding information from the audience. It's like a crossword puzzle or an anagram or what you like."

What Hitchcock did was to use knowledge to achieve suspense.

"Suspense is giving information to the audience. In other words, the audience must be told who the murderer is so when they see him associating with, say, a young woman, they want to say, 'Be careful! Don't go with him. We know. You don't.' In other words, they're ahead of the other characters. And that's what suspense is, you see."

Hitchcock always pooh-poohed the notion of any great intellectual content in his films. Yet he always made them lifelike, unpredictable, the horror incongruous.

"You know, I've always believed in murder by the babbling brook, in beautiful sunshine and lots of flowers, and that kind of thing."

In *North by Northwest,* Cary Grant is pursued in an open field by a crop-duster plane that shoots at him.

"And, of course, I did that to avoid the cliché. The cliché when you put a man on the spot is to have him standing under a street lamp at night, with all sorts of eerie atmospheres . . . black cats slithering along, wet streets, faces peering through curtains. . . . In the old days all intended to work the audience into a nervous condition. But I decided that that was old-hat and it was a cliché. So I said I will do it in bright sunshine— not a house or a tree, nowhere to hide, and no sign of the menace from anywhere."

In a way, Hitchcock used to say, his pictures were all comedies.

"I mean, one couldn't make a picture like *Psycho* without a sense of humor, because one knows ahead of time that you're going to put the audience through the wringer. Which is an amusing thought because you can hear them screaming."

Seeing a Hitchcock movie was like having a crazy nightmare, except that he was in control.

"It would be like if I were a man building a roller coaster. And I'd say, 'Well, I'm going to make that first dip go, and they'll scream like hell.' And people do, you see."

Hitchcock was an artist, and it was he who said of television that it brought murder into the home, where it belongs.

Rockwell

Somewhere, stored deep in the psyche of this country, there is a picture, like a faded snapshot, of the way we were. America before the freeways. Country churches and schoolhouses, kind hearts and gentle people.

Something in us remembers that which we have lost—or, perhaps, never experienced first hand. But the picture is there. And in the lower right-hand corner of it, in a familiar script, there is the name: Norman Rockwell. Rockwell died last night at his house in the Berkshires at the age of eighty-four.

He kept on painting until fairly recently, but the small-town, rural America with which he will always be associated passed on long before he did. Indeed, the old *Saturday Evening Post* (so many of whose covers he drew) had gone and left him a survivor.

"You know, doing *Saturday Evening Post* I had all my neighbors posing for me. But then I was doing, you know, the way I felt America."

The way Norman Rockwell felt America was the way America felt itself. It was a place of apple-cheeked kids and sweet old grandmothers, family dinners and Thanksgiving, old-fashioned country doctors and little boys fishing or dipping a little girl's pigtails in the inkwell.

"I was right up to here in corn. You know, I really . . . well, it was because I was corny. I was born on 103rd Street and Amsterdam Avenue. How corny can you get? You know!"

He told us in an interview back in the sixties that the critics were right about his paintings being superficial. Of course he'd depicted American motherhood, he said.

"'Cause I love American motherhood. I know. No, but I kind of done that thing, and people don't believe it any more. Freud spoiled everything in a way, didn't he? You know, didn't he?"

At one time, his own son painted and wouldn't put the name Rockwell on his work.

"He signs his name Jarvis. He doesn't sign his name Rockwell. The one thing, if you want to insult him, you say, 'Oh, you're the son of Norman Rockwell.' Then he vomits, you see, and this isn't so good."

Even though, after the *Post* died, he did more "problem" paintings—less idealized ones—he could never shake the image that he was the one who painted not the real America, but the one we all thought we remembered.

"Well, I'm an American, and I just saw people and maybe I found their soul. . . . Well, there's a little bit, but not really. I painted what I wanted to paint. In other words, it wouldn't have been any good. . . . You can't fool people for forty-seven years, you know. What did Lincoln say, ' . . . some of the people some of the time . . . all of the people some of the time, but not all of the people all of the time?' You know . . . and that's the way it is."

His posters and calendars look down on us still, from one corner of this country to the other. Rockwell never claimed to be a great artist with highly creative and original ideas. Yet he was hugely successful, financially.

"I'm on easy street, and so why don't I paint? Why? What is this thing in my soul that I don't paint? I don't want to paint that. I want to paint something that, you know, that somebody says to paint. Paint it. And I want to please them. I'm just not a fine-arts man. That's all there is to it. I'm an illustrator. And that's the way I'm gonna die."

Even in the teeming cities, even in the shopping malls off the screaming interstates, Americans think we remember a happier day. Perhaps we do. Or perhaps what we remember is Norman Rockwell.

Franco

Franco was a Fascist. He did things his way, he got his way. Despite his identification with Hitler, the fact is that although Hitler helped him a great deal, he hardly helped Hitler at all.

He was tough and stubborn. It took him a long time to take power in Spain. He held power for a long time, and it took him a long time to die. The doctors' bulletin announcing Generalissimo Franco's death this morning listed the physical ailments he's been fighting for so long—Parkinson's disease, coronary disease, ulcers, hemorrhaging, peritonitis, kidney failure, thrombophlebitis, pneumonia, endotoxic shock—until finally, a few hours ago, the heartbeat stopped, the brain waves recorded on the electroencephalogram flattened out. He was dead.

Many Americans didn't like Franco. He was not our sort of guy, but we more than lived with him; we helped him in exchange for bases. The American government was willing to do business with him when our NATO allies would not. They would not let Spain in NATO as long as Franco was in power. Critics have charged that American aid helped to keep Franco in power. They questioned whether what America got in return was worth the price.

Once upon a time, Hitler and Mussolini wanted the same thing. They had helped Francisco Franco tremendously during the Spanish Civil War, between 1936 and 1939. Italy had given Franco the planes he needed to cross the Straits of Gibraltar when he was headquartered in Morocco. Germany had provided warplanes, bombs, and guns to enable him to defeat the Republicans. Hitler and Mussolini felt that Franco owed them a great debt. They hoped to collect that debt during World War II. What happened was that Franco declared Spain nonbelligerent. He did allow German tankers to use the bays along the coast for refueling submarines and relaying intelligence information to the Axis about Allied ships passing through the Straits of Gibraltar. But he never did enter the war the way

Hitler had every reason to believe he would. Franco kept putting him off.

On October 23, 1941, there was a meeting between the *Caudillo* and the Führer at Undie, on the French side of the Spanish-French border. Hitler arrived first, and paced up and down for an hour on the station platform. One version has it that Franco purposely kept Hitler waiting, deliberately delaying his own arrival. According to that story, an assistant tried to hurry Franco and Franco told him the man who is kept waiting is the man who loses his temper, his calm, and his control.

Germany wanted to go in and take over Gibraltar, even thought about invading Spain, if necessary, to do so. But Franco wanted no part of letting Germany in. When the meeting finally got under way, it was Hitler who did almost all the talking. Franco listened without committing himself for hours—all afternoon, into the night—but Hitler could not get what he wanted. Franco evaded, resisted, on several occasions asked the translator to keep repeating some long argument of Hitler's, explaining he had not understood. Hitler was supposed to have jumped to his feet at one point as if to explode, but he never did. Instead, he accepted the loose agreement: Franco would come into the war someday (he didn't say when) and Germany would send supplies to Spain. As the war went on, Franco saw less and less reason to let the "someday" arrive.

Mussolini met with him and also came away without what he wanted. Some volunteers, the so-called Blue Division, did help the Germans on the Eastern Front. Franco took the position that he was fighting Communism against the Russians, but was neutral—vigilantly neutral, he said—in the Axis' war against Britain and the U.S.A.

President Harry S. Truman, on August 23, 1945, said at a news conference, "None of us like Franco or his government." And Adolf Hitler (the man who had helped Franco so much and expected so much), upon the suggestion of another meeting with the *Caudillo,* is quoted as having said, "I would prefer having three or four of my teeth pulled."

Brudno

The Pentagon put out some casualty figures for the Vietnam War this morning. Combat fatalities: nearly forty-six thousand. Other fatalities, nonhostile cause: over ten thousand. Yet even these figures are incomplete. They do not, for example, include Air Force Captain Ed Brudno.

Air Force Captain Edward A. Brudno is dead. He would have had a birthday today. He would have been thirty-three. But Ed Brudno is dead. He was found yesterday at his in-laws' house in Harrison, New York—a plastic bag tied over his head. Suicide, police say, although Dr. Henry Ryan, the coroner, won't issue a final report until tomorrow, when some tests have been completed.

HENRY RYAN: "That a thirty-three-year-old should be found dead in bed is surprising, always, to me. And, as I say, the result of our final investigation in various cases turns up some surprising things . . . heart disease, things of this nature. We just have to wait and see."

The death of Ed Brudno will not go down as a Vietnam War casualty, though maybe that's what it was. Pentagon records give only the broadest outline, scarcely revealing the person that was Ed Brudno.

PENTAGON SPOKESMAN: "Captain Brudno, who returned to the United States February 17 for homecoming processing at Westover Air Force Base, is survived by his widow, Deborah. The captain, who entered the Air Force in April 1963, was flying from an Air Base in Thailand, on October 18, 1965, when his F-4C Phantom fighter was downed over North Vietnam. The captain, born in Quincy, Massachusetts, was a 1963 graduate of MIT in Cambridge, Massachusetts."

Brudno had bounded off the homecoming plane. I saw a videotape of him this morning—smiling, shaking hands, saluting the officers who greeted him back in February. At Westover Air Force Base in Massachusetts, where he had his processing, they didn't realize he was so deeply troubled.

WESTOVER SPOKESMAN: "I had talked with him here on one occasion, and I found him to be very cheerful and happy to be home and we had nothing of that nature that we recognize here."

And yet, to Dr. Richard S. Wilbur, the Assistant Secretary of Defense for Health and Environment, the suicide of Ed Brudno—if that is what it was—comes as no great surprise.

RICHARD WILBUR: "This is what we had known from previous experience. Men who'd been in Japanese prison camps, men who'd been in Korean prison camps ... that during the first three years they are back they have a much greater possibility of dying from suicide, from homicide, or just through accident than do men who've been overseas the same length of time but who haven't been prisoners. So this is just the type of tragedy which we feared might happen."

Back in February, when the good news arrived that Ed was coming home, we spoke with his father, Dr. James Brudno.

JAMES BRUDNO: "His first letter that did come through after many, many months of captivity ... and he said that he was shot down and he injured his back ... he was cut in many places, and particularly in his face. He was then walked or marched all the way to Hanoi, where he was then confined."

People had been kind, Dr. Brudno told us four months ago. They remembered Ed all those long years he was gone.

JAMES BRUDNO: "Neighboring churches have had candles and prayers for my son. My son was known through the city and everybody liked him. My wife and I couldn't have had a better son."

Eight years ago, after Ed was shot down, his family feared that he was dead. And in a sense they were right.

Pablo Casals

Pablo Casals, who has died in Puerto Rico at the age of ninety-six, was a master cellist and also a conductor.

It is important, of course, that we pay attention to what the politicians and the generals are saying this morning. It may affect our lives. But also, just this once, we might pay attention to the passing of a musician. . . .

When Franco's Fascists took over in Spain, Casals had removed a national treasure from that country: himself. In thirty-four years of self-imposed exile in Prague and then in Puerto Rico, he gave that treasure to the world—playing, conducting, teaching.

In many ways, Pablo Casals was a simple man. It was the simplicity of genius. For, to him, a piece of music was an expression of the human spirit.

"That we are one of the leaves of a tree and the tree is all humanity. We can't live being a leaf, without the others, without the tree and without . . . we are only a leaf. Now we must think of the whole thing, by intelligence. By intelligence, and naturally, when there is intelligence there is love."

Alden Whitman's obituary in *The New York Times* this morning begins with the story of a cello student struggling with a suite by Bach. "I think it goes like this," the student said. "Don't think," replied the master. "It is better to feel."

149

Ed Cole

Ed Cole drove his twin-engine plane through a heavy rainstorm yesterday and it crashed south of Kalamazoo, Michigan, and he was killed. Ed Cole was a very special person.

Edward N. Cole had taken over just two months ago as chairman and chief executive officer of the Checker Motor Company, the tiny car maker that's famous for its taxicabs. They were delighted to get Ed, because he knew a little bit about running car companies. Until a few years ago he'd been president of General Motors. He retired from GM when he was sixty-five, and since then has been trying to get the world's biggest airplane off the ground as founder and chairman of International Huskey, Incorporated. And he worked on revolutionary car engines, including one in which gasoline would be replaced by a hydrazine fuel made out of water and air.

Ed never went to college. He'd always been crazy about cars, though, and after high school he enrolled in General Motors Institute. He left before graduating to take a job with the company's Cadillac Division. How could he resist the pay? Forty-five cents an hour! Later on, GM would pay him a quarter of a million dollars a year, but that was after he'd worked several miracles.

Just before the Korean War he was put in charge of building the Walker Bulldog tank. He found a plant for it in Cleveland. Now, not only was he full of beans, so was the plant. Thirty-nine million pounds of beans, to be exact. Cole had to go to court to get those beans removed. He used to fly himself around the country scrounging for machinery, but in ten months' time he managed to hire seven thousand workers to redesign the tank and get it into production.

They made him chief engineer at Chevrolet, and the Chevy engine was completely redesigned. Cole was always product-oriented, car-oriented. Nowadays, top executives in car companies (or in any corporation) tend to be financial and management wizards, but many of them don't really know the first thing about the products their companies are supposed to be all about. Not Ed. He had eighteen major patents to his credit. Some top executives stay in the rarefied atmosphere of their executive suites. Not Ed. You'd find him on the production floor, talking over problems with hourly workers. Nowadays, top executives tend to be soft-spoken, cool, methodical. Not Ed. He'd yell at you, pull you, prod you to get something done. Richard Gerstenber, the board chairman at GM, was once quoted as saying, "I guess you could describe Ed as the kind of guy to whom you might say, 'Ed, I'd like to move the General Motors building across the road,' and he'd say, 'Do you want it facing Second Avenue or the Boulevard?'"

Impatient, that was Ed Cole. Today's top execs tend not to jump into new ways of doing things. They tend to resist change. Not Ed. He designed the air-cooled, rear-engine Corvair. That was not one of his triumphs. An unknown young lawyer by the name of Ralph Nader wrote a book about it called *Unsafe at Any Speed.* Cole made his company look into rotary engines, made them spend money on development of the rotary. "See," some people will say, "that's what you get for being first." It was Cole who persuaded GM to use catalytic converters to meet antipollution standards, Cole who pushed for air bags when the whole industry was saying no.

Despite his business and his "busyness," Cole was a family man devoted to his wife, Dolly, and to their two children.

A few years ago, a week and a half before he retired from GM, Cole gave some public-service awards to some GM employees, and this is part of what he said:

" . . . retirement is fast approaching, and I know only too well that most of our formal careers have a fixed time span. You can only work so long at these careers. But there is no limit on a person's opportunity to serve his neighbors, his community, his nation outside of his regular job."

They say that Ed Cole was the last of a breed in American business, that they just don't make 'em like him any more. If that is true, it's too bad.

151

Bill Lear

What was it that Bill Lear had? This remarkable man, who has now died of leukemia at the age of seventy-five, had a lot of money, for one thing (about $75 million), people say. And he had hundreds of patents and inventions to his credit, including some extremely successful ones. But there wouldn't have been the money and there wouldn't have been the inventions if it weren't for some other things Lear had. A certain sense of restlessness, an unwillingness to let things be, and a zest for life.

If you're listening right now on a car radio, maybe the first thing we should tell you about Bill Lear is that he invented the car radio. That's right. He also was the first one to install a radio transmitter in an airplane, to make a radio that you could operate entirely off an electric line, without batteries. Lear was the one who thought up the first successful lightweight automatic pilot and automatic approach-control systems for planes, and the first successful automatic landing system for commercial jets.

Lear was the one who first came up with an eight-track stereo system for planes and cars and homes, and the one who made the first successful corporate-business jet airplane in the world: the Learjet.

One trouble with talking about a fellow like William P. Lear is that by the time you've finished listing all the stuff he did, you haven't got time to talk about who he was and what made him the way he was.

Imagine this kid in the public schools of Chicago, working in his spare time shining shoes and doing other odd jobs. He didn't get along with his mother, who had quite a temper, we're told, and who thought her son's inventive bent was just a waste of time and money. Lear would later say that he worked out a blueprint for himself when he was all of twelve years old. He resolved to make enough money so that he would never be stopped from finishing anything. And he knew that to accumulate money in a hurry (and he was in a hurry), he would have to invent something people wanted. He decided that if he was going to stand on his own feet, he was going to have to leave home. Which he did.

Lear quit school after the eighth grade to take a job as a mechanic. At sixteen he lied about his age and joined the Navy. He studied radio during World War I at the Great Lakes Naval Training Station. He gave up the Navy because at one point he decided it would just take him too long to become an admiral. He was on his way.

After he did invent the car radio in 1924, he founded his first company, the Radio Coil and Wire Corporation. He traded that in 1930 for a one-third interest in the Calvin Corporation, which was to become Motorola.

In 1934, RCA paid him a fortune for a simple radio amplifier that revolutionized the making of radio sets, and he used that stake to start Lear Incorporated, which produced the miniature cowl-flap motors for aircraft and filled $100 million worth of defense contracts in World War II. After that war he designed the first lightweight automatic pilot and approach-control systems, all of which preceded the Learjet, of course, and the stereo systems.

He'd go after a goal, and often, when he reached it, he'd sell out to start all over on something else. Sometimes he'd give up, but only after he decided to. That's what he decided about the steam car eight years ago, after he'd sunk seventeen million dollars into it. What was seventeen million dollars to him?

He loved to work. Eighteen hours a day was nothing to him. And he loved to play. Sometimes he'd stay up all night gambling, friends say. Not an easy man to keep up with day or night, on the job or at a crap game. He loved parties and Scotch and pretty women, and he deprived himself of none of them. "You know what I'd like?" he told an interviewer. "I want my youth back and not for the reason you think. I really want my youth back," he said, "so I can misspend it again."

Ralf Brent

Ralf Brent was still alive when this piece was broadcast. But
he was dying and he knew it was a kind of obituary.

Ralf Brent is a man who has always loved life and lived it with
zest. At play or at work, he was always in action. He was a
successful broadcaster, communicator, executive, and entrepre-
neur, who seemed to know everything and everybody, and knew
how to make things happen. And, as busy people often are, he
was called on to help in public causes, too. Ralf Brent recorded
some cancer announcements in the 1960s.

Now, at the age of sixty-two, Ralf Brent is dying. Not of
cancer, but of amyotrophic lateral sclerosis—Lou Gehrig's disease. In the year he's had it, ALS has robbed him of his speech
and most of the use of his legs, arms, and fingers. But his mind
is unaffected by the disease that has ravaged his body. And even
now you will find him in his Manhattan apartment, working,
writing a book ever so slowly, yet with a sense of urgency. He
writes:

> I better get to this, because I realize that the time for writ-
> ing is growing short. How I wish I could still type a
> hundred words a minute. I have so much to tell you. If
> you're like me, you never heard of ALS. But it's not Lou
> Gehrig fighting for his life and losing, it's me, fighting
> back against a disease that so far produces one hundred
> percent fatality. There's no chemotherapy, no X-ray treat-
> ment, no surgery, no exercises that help as in other
> diseases.

Ralf Brent's way of fighting back is to organize, to use those
contacts of his to make sure people will know about ALS, a
disease about as common as muscular dystrophy. Through
those contacts, he's raising money to fund a new clinic at New
York's Mount Sinai Hospital, the first such clinic anywhere for
ALS patients.

Even now, though he can't talk any more, he is on the executive committee of an ALS foundation whose offices he walked into a year ago and said, "You people are lucky. I'm dying of ALS and I know how this town works, and let's get going." And sure enough, he's been responsible for getting space for ALS ads in major magazines.

Now, though, Ralf spends most of his time in his apartment, writing the book.

I keep insisting that people treat me like a person, the person they knew. And I get pretty angry when they don't. But it occurred to me today, maybe I'm not acting like one. And I wonder if I'm not role-playing the part of a dying man. Okay, so it's more comfortable to let your head hang down, but as of today, I'm going to look more like the person I'd like to be treated as.

This summer, the family took a beach house on the Jersey Shore, and Ralf's sons, or a nurse, would carry him down to the water's edge to feel the sea breeze in his face again and watch the rhythmic lapping of the waves. He writes:

I don't feel that what someone said to me the other day, 'It isn't fair what's happening to you,' is true at all. I told my friend, 'Don't say that. I have had almost everything a person could hope for—marriage, three children, boats, houses, travel, money. I paint. I write. I love music, beauty.' Suppose I was a poor black in the Bronx and had ALS. Then it wouldn't be fair—to have nothing and then get ALS.

So writes Ralf Brent. It is not easy for him any more to go to the beach or to a concert. But he can listen to the sounds of the New York Philharmonic drift up to his balcony from Central Park. He has written:

Just because the time is short, and they've told you so, does that change the purpose of my life? Why did I really want to learn, to accomplish anything at any time of my life if it only ended in death. And each thought, each word of mine, I believe, changes the rest of the world for all, for all time. So I must be responsible. I have been. I must continue to be until my time comes. It is not up to me to choose that time.

Whatever our situation, we should make the most of life. We should savor every second of it. That's what Ralf Brent has always believed. And it is clear it is what he believes now.

When heavy seas let up a bit,
The news will never stop.
But fish that are a little weird
Come swimming to the top.

Light News Day

On Letting Well Enough Alone

One of the nice things about the world is that everything keeps improving all the time. Have you noticed that? The urge never to let well enough alone has brought us ever newer and ever more improved products and services. The latest of these comes from the Postal Service. It wants to improve the Zone Improvement Program, otherwise known as the Zip system, by adding four more digits to the present five-digit codes, so the Postal Service can be even more wonderful and improved than it is already. And you and I will have the chance to improve our memories by remembering nine Zip digits instead of five: 076434291, let us say.

A hundred and twenty-five years ago, when Otis invented the elevator, an improvement was really an improvement. The elevator was a good idea, although the doctors now tell us that walking up and down the stairs used to be good for people. But at some point they improved the elevator by replacing the elevator operator with buttons so that you can run the elevator yourself.

A lot of improvements are that way. The phone company thinks it is a great improvement that you now place your own long-distance calls, instead of having an operator do it. A major airline is now promoting a terrific improvement in baggage handling—you carry your bags on and off the plane yourself.

Just when you think that they've about run out of improvements, along comes another one. As you know, Amtrak, which was created to improve railroad passenger service, has improved passenger railroad service so much that there hardly is any passenger railroad service any more. Every time Amtrak comes along with what it calls an improvement, it means cutting out more service and reducing the number of passenger trains and cities served.

And the Postal Service, which has done all that it has done so far in the name of improvement, now routes mail all over creation to get it from Point A to Point B. It makes fewer deliveries a day, proposes fewer delivery days in the week, and often takes a letter longer to get from here to there than it used to, but at greatly increased cost (of course). My, it's just an inspiration the way those folks have improved things.

Food is greatly improved now, as you well know. Tomatoes, for example, have been improved so much that they now have no taste at all and a texture like cardboard. Clothes have been so improved, what with doubleknit polyesters and all, that a whole new family of products has emerged to deal with static cling. Why, almost every area you can think of has been improved. With the benefit of electronics and audiovisual aids, with sophisticated professional teaching techniques, we have so improved the educational system in this country that some of our college students don't even need to take the improved remedial reading courses that universities now offer. The improved, hand-held calculators mean kids don't need to add and subtract any more. Good thing, too, since they can't.

Government has really improved, as the candidates running for office down through the years have assured us it would. It's just hard to imagine how everybody got along without the agencies and bureaus that we now have to improve things. Congress is in there improving away, session after session. Expensive? Sure, but look at how improved it all is. Streamlined, too. And efficient. That's why we have GSA to streamline and improve the way government agencies do things and, of course, to make sure everything is on the up and up. Taxes, especially, are up and up.

Sometimes you get obstructionists who want to stand in the way of improvement and progress. There'll always be somebody who doesn't want to have to use two hands to use his digital watch; who does not find easy-opening cans that easy to open; who prefers country roads to superhighways; who can't stand all the convenience provided by convenience household appliances.

There are even some people who don't prefer the way television has improved and would rather sit and talk or read a book. But there's no stopping progress. Excelsior! Onward and upward, ad infinitum. Or is it ad nauseum?

In a Handbasket

Things are looking up. That Pollyannish thesis may seem an odd one, given the way the news has been going, but we are prepared to defend the proposition with some more examples of improvement.

There's no need to cite the various ways in which the world is going to hell in a handbasket. The news is full of those. What we should like to do here this morning, for just a few minutes, is to find you some things that are better than they used to be, or promise to be better one of these days.

Scientific research has shown that maximum alertness and concentration are possible only when a person has warm feet and a cool head. Warm feet can be had with electric socks, which are not new, but until now there has been no device to assure you of having a cool head. Well, a Japanese inventor by the name of Hiroshi Majima has come up with something he says should be ideal for presidents, officers, professors, students, all intellectual people, and all good safety drivers. Those are his words. His invention is called Majima's Electronic Head Cooler. It's a three-and-a-half-ounce headband with a cooling element and a cord that can be plugged into your house current or into the cigarette lighter outlet in your car. The device sells for $160. The world is sure to be better off with fewer hot heads around. You have to admit that.

Science keeps plugging away, finding out things we didn't know before. The English magazine *Weekend* reports that people who work on the upper floors of skyscrapers are much more likely to fall in love than people who work on the lower floors. Only two out of ten people working on the lower floors of skyscrapers were found to be romantically linked to people in the same offices. On the upper floors it was more like nine out of ten. In the middle floors it was four or five out of ten. Apparently, people whose feet are on the ground don't fall in love as readily as those whose heads are in the clouds. Information such as this is sure to make this a better world, isn't it? No wonder things are looking up.

New Jersey doesn't have a state song, and Assemblyman Richard Visocki plans to sponsor a resolution naming Bruce Springsteen's "Born to Run" as the New Jersey state song. Now, you can see why a politician might be fond of a song entitled "Born to Run," but the lyrics of that particular song say, "Baby, this town rips the bones from your back. It's a death trap. It's a suicide rap. We gotta get out while we're young. . . ." With that as state song, New Jersey will get better. It's bound to.

Richard Zawadski, a British computer consultant, has built an electronic nanny to improve baby raising. ORCA III, with tape drives and typewriter keys, tells the Zawadski's daughter, Gemma, bedtime stories, soothes her when she cries, and will teach her English, French, and German when she starts to talk, he says. No, it can't change her diapers. You can't have everything, you know.

And movies are better than ever. Proof is the film festival to run in New York City next month. The twenty-five most abominable films ever made. Lauren Drury, one of the festival promoters, says the directing, sets, scriptwriting, and acting all have to be terrible in order for a film to qualify. Along with *Santa Claus Conquers the Martians*, *They Saved Hitler's Brain*, and *The Attack of the Killer Tomatoes*, the schedule calls for the showing of the 1938 film classic *The Terror of Tiny Town* (which is billed as the world's only musical Western with an all-midget cast). No doubt about it, things are looking up.

Some News Is Good, and Some Is Worse, and Some News Goes from Bad ... to Verse.

Maybe you've heard about some of this already, but then again, maybe you haven't. Here comes a contingent of lawyers (or is it a delegation or maybe a lamentation of lawyers ...) before the Federal Trade Commission in Washington. The lawyers are there to argue that the Anheuser-Busch Brewing Company should not be allowed to use the word "natural" in describing its beers, since those beers contain certain things like tannic acid and chemically treated beechwood chips. And why, you may wonder, is the client of these lawyers saying these nasty things about Anheuser-Busch? The answer is the Miller Brewing Company, which has already argued before the Bureau of Alcohol, Tobacco, and Firearms that its competitor, Busch, should not be permitted to call its Michelob Light Beer "light," since it contains 134 calories.

Well, things are not always what they are called anyway, as you have very likely found out in your own life. You know the Bay City Rollers, the rock musicians? Well, they are not from Bay City, Michigan, at all. They are, in fact, Scottish. When they were organized, they just happened to be looking for an American-sounding name. One of them blindfolded himself and stuck a pin in a map and it happened to hit Bay City, Michigan. They have since been to Bay City and they did get a terrific welcome there. But now, perhaps in the interest of truth in packaging, they have decided to drop the words "Bay City" from their name altogether. From now on they will simply be known as the Rollers.

If that makes you mad, you may wish to purchase the services of Dr. Nasty. Dr. Nasty is not his real name, either, but he operates out of Manchester, Connecticut, and for a fee (ten dollars for twenty-five words or less) will write a poison-pen letter to anybody that you want to have a poison-pen letter written to for whatever reason.

In Manchester, Connecticut,
For those whose sense of etiquette

163

Won't let them curse or vent their spleen
Or speak in words the least bit mean,
This man for just a ten-buck fee
Will be as mean as he can be.
And write a note to curl the hair
Of whomever it is out there
You wish to castigate or blame.
Dr. Nasty's not his name.
But he who turns out letters hot
To use his real name, better not.
But point him to the girl or guy—
Tell him who and what and why—
And he'll compose for that one's eyes
A letter they will just despise.

In Trinidad, I've heard it said,
The mailboxes are painted red.
And in New York the other day,
A visitor from down that way
Found a box of crimson hue
And did what you might think she'd do.
She dropped two letters in the slot,
Then pulled the handle, like as not.
Then (here comes the part that shocks)
A voice came from within the box.
That's what a New York firebox does.
It asked her where the fire was.
A fireman got her back her letter.
The next time, she says, she'll know better.

And finally, there has been born
A new and different kind of corn.
A man named Walton Galinat of Milton, Mass.,
Says he has got a special breed of corn up there
The ear of which in shape is square.
A scientist who works with seeds,
He says square corn is what this world needs
To help us in our present state,
For square corn will not roll off your plate.

A Little Humor There

The average blue-collar worker with a wife and a couple of kids made more money in 1979 than he made the year before. However, that money would not buy for him anywhere near as much as the less money he made before. In fact, when you figure inflation in, that average American worker actually took a pay cut last year of 7.9 percent. And this year is even worse. Everybody's expenses are going up faster than his real income is going down, and now we know what the Pennsylvania Dutch mean by that old saying, "The hurrier I go, the behinder I get." You've got to have a sense of humor to get along in today's world.

There are two kinds of humor (at least) growing out of the news. There's the stuff that just happens, without anybody trying to be funny. For example, Eric Nystrom of Des Moines, Iowa, had to apply for a new state income tax refund check because his dog, Alice, ate the original check for $195.16 when it came in. Maybe the seven-month-old basset hound was trying to be funny. I suppose there's no way of telling.

But Rip Howell, a geology student at the University of Southwestern Louisiana, is trying to be funny, no doubt about that. He thought up a way to outdo somebody he had heard about in Alabama who sat in a tub of chocolate pudding for twenty-eight hours. Howell's idea is to sit in a tub of ketchup for thirty-four hours. And if he holds out until six o'clock tonight, he will make it. Billing himself as "The Human French Fry," Howell poured thirty-one gallons of ketchup into a tub and got in, wearing only his shorts and some Vaseline smeared on the parts of him he intends to keep submerged. He has been in there since eight o'clock yesterday morning. Howell says he just wanted to do something that nobody had ever done before.

Things seem funny or don't seem funny depending, at least in part, on your situation. A lot of humor grows out of adversity, and a Russian humorist who has emigrated from the Soviet Union has written what amounts to a joke book of current funniness behind the iron curtain. Emil Draitser, now a professor of Russian literature at UCLA, calls his book *Forbidden Laughter,* and it includes some jokes smuggled out through coded letters from some of his former fellow humorists in the Soviet Union. There is not just advertent and inadvertent humor, there is also dangerous humor—the kind that makes fun of the regime—like this joke implying Brezhnev's senility: Brezhnev shows up at some Kremlin function wearing a yellow shoe and a black shoe. "Do not worry, Comrade Chairman," says an aide, "we will send the chauffeur for other shoes." Says Brezhnev, "That won't help. The other pair looks just like these." Take my babushka, please. Or the one about Brezhnev and the cosmonauts: "The Americans were the first to land on the moon, so we will be the first to land on the sun," Brezhnev says. But the cosmonauts protest, "Comrade, we'll be burned to death!" And Brezhnev reassures them, "Do you think we know nothing? We arranged for you to land at night." And this one, the latest gag from Afghanistan, says Draitser: Why are our troops staying so long in Afghanistan? Answer: They are still looking for the people who invited them.

One Man's Meat

Just remember this: Every silver lining has a cloud.

Everybody was thrilled (right?) when Maxie and Kris Anderson completed their transcontinental balloon flight, coming down safe and sound on a tree farm in the Gaspé Peninsula. Well, not *everybody*. Rosaire Plourde was not thrilled. He happens to own the tree farm, and says he's going to keep the balloon until somebody pays him for the damage to his property. No, says Plourde, it was not the balloon that did the damage. It was the four-wheel-drive vehicles driven by all those reporters that dug up a section of his road.

Ralph Davis's story is an inspiring one. In a way. He is now a county commissioner in Hawkins County, Tennessee. But forty years ago he was a fugitive from justice. Seems he was sentenced to sixty days in jail for some misdemeanor. And when he was about to start serving his term, the jailer let him run home for a few personal items. Davis did not run home. He ran away (to Maryland) and stayed there for thirty years. Then, in 1970, he figured bygones would be bygones and returned to Tennessee, where he became well known and liked enough to run for public office and get elected. And so, a happy ending.

But wait! That's the silver lining. Now comes the cloud. A criminal-court judge, James Beckner, now says the state has a duty to enforce the old sentence that Davis ran away from. Even though he's now seventy-one years old, he may have to serve those sixty days in the hoosegow.

It is spring, of course, and boys will be boys. A seventeen-year-old Oklahoma boy took himself for a joy ride in a truck that wasn't his yesterday. His silver lining did not last long, however. He collided with a highway patrol car and dragged it for half a mile. Trooper Tom Fitzgibbon was not injured, and he did finally catch the kid. The truck, incidentally, turned out to be filled with coffins.

And birds will be birds, building their nests so nicely and all, this time of year. Ah, yes, whatever else may be wrong with the world, at least that silver lining is intact. Except in Honolulu, where this one bird used a cigarette butt in his nest under the eaves of a duplex. The cloud behind that particular silver lining was a cloud of smoke. The cigarette was still smoldering, apparently, and the result was that the house burned down. Nobody was injured, but there was $25,000 worth of damage.

Now, a good cat might have prevented all that from happening. But not necessarily. In Salina, Kansas, yesterday, a cat (perhaps in pursuit of some bird that meant to set a house afire) climbed a power line, made contact with some high-voltage lines, and knocked out electric power to two hundred homes.

In Omaha, Mayor Al Veys wanted to make several thousand phone calls to citizens to urge them to vote for an increase in the sales tax at the polls today. The silver lining was that he didn't have to make those calls personally. An automatic device called 3,500 people every twelve hours for him to play his recorded message. The cloud was that the machine did not quit at 9:00 P.M. when it was supposed to, and several thousand Omaha phones rang last night in the middle of the night and in the wee hours of this morning. Not exactly the way to win votes and influence people.

So look for the silver lining. Silver linings are allowed.
But behind each silver lining, you may find another cloud.

News Bulletin from the Front Yard

Around here, in a busy newsroom, we get to thinking of the world in terms of war and peace, power and politics. We think of cycles in terms of business cycles, inflation and recession, numbers marching one way or another and somehow dragging us along with them.

But it is a Friday morning in April and where I am right now, and in a lot of other places in the North Temperate Zone, a miracle is taking place under our very noses. And if we don't notice it, well, we're just not paying attention. To every thing there is a season, and this is the season of flowers.

Once upon a time there were no flowers on this earth. The planet is about four billion years old, remember, and as recently as one hundred million years ago, you wouldn't have found a single blossom.

But just before the age of reptiles came to a close, something happened, something wonderful and important. The angiosperms emerged. The way plants used to reproduce themselves, little sperm cells would wriggle their way through the dew and the raindrops, and then seeds without flowers evolved. The wind carried pollen from one plant to another. That was before there were birds singing in the forest, before mammals had exploded on the scene. The birds and the mammals had to wait, you see, for the age of flowers. And later the insects, birds, and other animals would help flowers to spread around the planet. But we're getting ahead of ourselves.

The first flower came into existence sometime before the last dinosaur had died. Loren Eisley, the late poet and naturalist, wrote: "The flower must have bloomed on some raw upland, was wind-pollinated like its early pine cone relatives, and was inconspicuous."

No poets were around to notice at the time. Eisley says it must have been a profound innovation in the world of life. The true flowering plant grew a seed in the heart of a flower, a seed initiated by fertilizing pollen grains, a fully equipped embryonic plant packed in a little enclosed box full of nutritious food. Talk about innovations in packaging. This meant that plants could travel as never before. They developed tantalizing nectars and pollens and sweet berries to attract the birds and the bees.

Specialized groups of insects evolved to feed on the new sources the plants afforded. So the flower figures importantly in evolution, not only in the plant world, but in the animal world as well. Instead of the cold, dark, monotonous green that existed before, now there was this dazzling profusion of color.

So now, when you and I step outdoors on an April morning, there may be Virginia bluebells and daffodils to greet us, hyacinth and wild columbine.

Outside my front door there is a blooming magnolia tree that's bigger than the house. Not to notice that, or to think it's not important, I'd have to be not only insensitive but blind.

We're a highly evolved species, we *Homo sapiens*. We have a lot on our minds these days, a lot to worry about. But we're also part of nature, part of a universe of miracles, all connected somehow. Frances Thompson, the English poet, once wrote that "One cannot pluck a flower without troubling a star."

If this old planet didn't spin,
We'd all be so much rubble.
But love's what makes the world go 'round,
And that's why we're in trouble.

Love

Was an empty and meaningless kind of a sham.
But Matuzak's arrested and charged with a scam.

As for Kyle, whom he loved, though they never had kissed,
Only now does Reed realize she doesn't exist.
As a hobby Reed builds and collects little boats,
And he has extra time that these days he devotes
To his model collection. And he points with a smile
To a tugboat. Its nameplate: the U.S.S. *Kyle*.

Where Have You Gone, Mike DiMaggio

It was quite a wedding as weddings go,
The wedding of Mike DiMaggio
To his sweetheart, Kyri. A girl, a boy,
And their friends there in Berwyn, Illinois.
The wedding reception on Saturday night
Was something that really went out of sight.

The wedding cake and the champagne bubble—
The fun they all had before the trouble!
The family and two hundred guests in all
Who were there at the local Elks Club hall.
Just another reception in that big room.
Another toast to a bride and groom.

The people laugh and the glasses clink,
And the corks go pop and the people drink,
And the music plays and the people dance
To songs of happiness and romance.
Who'd think that by some unpredictable quirk
Everybody would go berserk?

A wedding is a time of joy.
And there in Berwyn, Illinois,
Michael and Kyri DiMaggio
Invited their families, and friends they know,
To the wedding to see them tie the knot.
And they asked the people they loved a lot
To the wedding reception, one and all,
Saturday night at the Elks Club hall.

Everything went according to plan.
The toast was made by the groom's best man.
The champagne flowed and the music played
And expressions of love and good wishes were made.

The in-laws chatted and beamed with pride,
And people lined up to kiss the bride.

The wedding cake was a baker's dream.
Looking back, what a shame it now would seem
That nobody got to eat the cake.
They really couldn't, for goodness' sake,
For suddenly, on this special night,
Out of nowhere there came a fight—
More like a nightmare than real, true life.
Somebody danced with an usher's wife.

It was, according to Kyri's mother,
The bridegroom's fifteen-year-old brother.
The usher swung at the nervy kid,
And the kid swung back, is what he did.
And someone came to the usher's aid,
And a few insulting remarks were made.

The coats came off and fists then flew.
The altercation just somehow grew,
With chairs and bottles and glasses there,
And food that flew through the evening air.
The Elks Club manager called a cop
To try to bring it all to a stop.

And what officers found there on the scene
Was a situation rather mean.
The chaos now was so complete
That the fight had spread out into the street.

Reinforcements were called for then:
Thirty-five more law enforcement   n
From two other local suburbar   1s.
And these people dressed ur   (s and gowns
Were covered by now (if   1 be told)
With sauce from the r   res, hot and cold,

And the icing and crumbs from the wedding cake
That cost hundreds of dollars, for heaven's sake.

Broken glass littered the Elks hall floor.
People streamed in and out the door.
There's a hole in the wall, in the very wall
Of that major room in the Elks Club hall.
A hole you would spot—it could not be missed—
Made by a bottle, or someone's fist.

Twelve people were hurt by the time it ceased . . .
Hospital-treated, and then released.
And other celebrants, family and guests,
Were numbered among the twelve arrests.

The couple is now on their honeymoon,
A honeymoon in the month of June.
But they couldn't take off right away,
For first, the bride had to wait to pay
The money set for the bridegroom's bail
To get him out of the Berwyn jail.

Mike swears what happened was not his fault.
He is charged, however, with assault.
I think it is probably safe to say
That they'll never forget their wedding day
As the time goes by and the years pass.
Those wedding pictures should be a gas.

POSSLQ

Rich as it is, the English language does not have a word for everything. For example, for years now it's been evident that there is no good word to describe, much less to introduce (at a party, say), the person with whom one is living. One's roommate, as it were, of the opposite sex, with whom one has not exchanged marital vows.

How does a young woman introduce George? My lover, George? No, that's out. My boyfriend? Definitely dated. My friend? My fiancé? No, "friend" is ambiguous, and "fiancé" suggests an engagement, which may or may not be applicable.

We haven't had a good word for a partner in such a relationship until now. I'm grateful to William Rukeyser over at *Money* magazine for discovering the word, although he did not invent it. He found it by looking at some forms put out by the U.S. Bureau of the Census, which is preparing to do its 1980 nose count. There, as an acronym for "Persons of Opposite Sex Sharing Living Quarters," was the word POSSLQ. POSSLQ, the very word we've been looking for. Precise, to the point, and so much more businesslike than, say, "honeybunch," or "sweet potato pie." You can say, without so much as a blush, "This is DeeDee, my POSSLQ." Or, "Say hello to Franklin. We're POSSLQS."

Language, like nature, abhors a vacuum. And since there has been no good word to cover the situation that used to be known as "living in sin," the folks over at the Census Bureau are making what is sure to be an invaluable contribution to our vocabulary—POSSLQ: Persons of Opposite Sex Sharing Living Quarters. So simple. So nonjudgmental. And in its own way, sort of poetic, too.

Come live with me and be my love,
And we will some new pleasures prove
Of golden sands and crystal brooks
With silken lines and silver hooks.

There's nothing that I wouldn't do
If you would be my POSSLQ.
You live with me, and I with you,
And you will be my POSSLQ.
I'll be your friend and so much more;
That's what a POSSLQ is for.

And everything we will confess;
Yes, even to the IRS.
Someday, on what we both may earn,
Perhaps we'll file a joint return.
You'll share my pad, my taxes joint.
You'll share my life—up to a point!
And that you'll be so glad to do,
Because you'll be my POSSLQ.

Come live with me and be my love,
And share the pain and pleasure of
The blessed continuity,
Official POSSLQuity.
And I will whisper in your ear
That word you love so much to hear.
And love will stay forever new,
If you will be my POSSLQ.

Occupation: Horsewife

This week (I hesitate to mention)
Somebody called to my attention
A little story out of Boulder.
I put it in my story folder
In case there should be something there
Worth using someday on the air.

It seems some fellow with bravado,
There in Boulder, Colorado,
Tried to make a point one day
In a rather novel sort of way.

Ross Howard is his name, and Ross,
Rented for himself a horse,
And took it 'round to City Hall,
Or rather what out there they call
The Office of the County Clerk,
To try his little scheme to work.

The office people nearly died
When Howard thereupon applied
For a marriage license, that he might wed.
"I am the groom," Ross Howard said,
"And I've got the bride right here, of course."
And he pointed to the rented horse.

It struck Ross Howard rather strange,
What seems to be a recent change
In Colorado's interpretation
Of the laws that govern the marriage station.

They're granting a wedding license there
To any adult applying pair.
To men and women fairly,
But, ah, not necessarily.

To women and women, to men and men,
Instead of the way it's always been.

And old Ross Howard it did vex
To have folks married to their own sex.
And so his gripe, this week he vented it,
And went and found this horse and rented it.
And took it 'round to the County Clerk's,
To the office where Clara Rorex works.

He said, in a voice that boomed and carried,
"This horse and I want to get married.
If a boy can marry a boy," he said,
"If a girl and a girl you let be wed,
Why, it seems to me it's only fair
That a cowboy should marry his favorite mare."

Now, challenge Miss Rorex never shirks,
So she called together the other clerks
And consulted them, and then said to Ross,
"We won't grant a license to wed this horse."
"All right," said he, "but I'll tell you what,
You have to explain to me why not."

"In the first place, sir," Miss Rorex said,
"This horse is much too young to wed.
On your application you clearly state
This little filly is only eight.

"You've got no blood test, nor do I see
What the law requires that there must be.
Of parental consent you have no proof.
Not so much as a horse's hoof.

"Nor can your intended say to you
The age-old promise of 'I do.'

In fact, if you will let me say,
She's much more likely to tell you 'Neigh.'

"The law, I'll tell you right out flat,
Is not as liberal as all that.
This is one wedding knot that will stay untied.
And your application is denied."

So into the sunset Howard rode,
In the traditional cowboy mode.
And it seems to me that although he lost,
He avoided paying an awful cost.

For suppose the Clerk's Office had told him yes,
Why, then he'd have been in an awful mess.
To be saddled for good with a wifely horse
Would have filled him, I'm sure, with great remorse.

Though a horse needs a groom, he'd have felt great wrath
If he'd led that horse down the bridal path.
It might well ruin a man's whole life
To have a horse as his wedded wife.

Something borrowed, something blue,
And the clippity-clop of a horse's shoe.
All those oats on the dinner table;
The house always looking like a stable.

A horse for a wife is no man's bag.
I'm sure she'd have turned out to be a nag.
And if I were married to any horse
I think I'd ask for a divorce.

Amiable Child

In the crowds and traffic and noise of the big city, it's easy for an individual life to get lost. But at the edge of all this, there is a little touch of humanity at a spot frozen in time.

There's usually a breeze up here, blowing in off the Hudson River. This was all farm country, once upon a time.

Imagine how it must have been, on the West Side of Manhattan, when a little boy by the name of St. Claire Pollock used to run and play on what was then his father's farm. Charles Pollock had settled overlooking the Hudson River, perhaps because it reminded him of the flowing rivers and green hills of his native Ireland.

One sad day in 1797, St. Claire Pollock, who was then only five years old, went out to play too close to the edge of a very steep embankment, and he fell and was killed. The family put up a little stone monument in his memory, and they stipulated that in any future sale of the property the buyers would have to agree that the stone marker would not be disturbed.

Years passed. The city and the nation grew. On what used to be the Pollock farm, the tomb of President Ulysses S. Grant now stands. The West Side Highway runs at the foot of the hill, Riverside Drive at the top. Riverside Church, with its graceful bell tower, is across the street. And now children run and play in what is part of Riverside Park.

So much has changed, but the breeze still blows off the river. And to this day you can still find, enclosed behind a tiny iron fence, a memorial in stone. Look ... a promise kept after all these years. It reads:

Erected to the Memory of an Amiable Child
St. Claire Pollock
Died 15 July 1797
In the fifth year of his age

When you do things by the numbers,
It's more accurate by far.
But you may forget, along the way,
Exactly who you are.

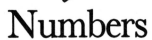

Numbers

Two Things Not to Worry About

The average American is an amazing fellow. The Bureau of the Census, which keeps tabs on the average American, now tells us that the average American is, at the present time, two years older than he was ten years ago. Think of that. Are you only two years older than you were ten years ago? Neither am I. But the average American is. In 1970 he was 27.9 years old, and in the statistics put out by the bureau over the weekend the average American is now 30.0 years old. How he does it I would sure like to know. I, for one, am ten years older than I was ten years ago.

And here's something else to think about. Have you ever seen a barrel of oil? I mean, we keep hearing about how OPEC has increased the price of a barrel of oil to such and such, so we think about barrels of oil a lot. But have you ever seen one? Of course you haven't, and neither has anybody else.

The fact that the average American is two years older than he was ten years ago, and the fact that neither you nor I have ever seen a barrel of oil, are related in the following way: neither exists. There's no such thing as the average American and there's no such thing as a barrel of oil.

Let me explain to you why there's no such thing as a barrel of oil and no such thing as the average American. First, the oil. Oil is sometimes contained in fifty-gallon drums. But that's not a barrel. A barrel (if there were such a thing) would be forty-two gallons. But nobody puts oil in forty-two-gallon containers. Since 1866, oil has been sold by the gallon. In that year some West Virginia producers decided to give their customers two extra gallons of oil for every forty they bought. And so the forty-two-gallon unit was born, although the standard container became the fifty-gallon drum. There are no barrels. Never were any barrels. The barrel of oil is a mythical beast, which is why you have never seen one, although possibly you have worried about barrels of oil, and particularly the price of a barrel of oil. Don't worry about it any more. There's just no point in worrying about something that doesn't exist.

Now, the average American. The Census Bureau says what happened in the last ten years is that the population under fourteen years of age decreased by fourteen percent, while those between twenty-five and thirty-four increased by thirty-nine percent and those aged sixty-five or older increased by twenty-four percent. Fewer babies, more old folks, and a lot more middle-aged, and you wind up with the average age of the population: a nice, round 30.0.

I think the way you arrive at this is to total up all the ages of everybody in the country and divide that by the size of the population. Or maybe what you do is find the age at which half the population is older than you and the other half is younger than you. I'm not sure which, but in either case you can be sure of one thing. The average American (the one who has aged two years in the last ten years) achieved this remarkable record by the simple expedient of not existing. Like the barrel of oil he is the figment of some statistician's imagination. The average human being in the world is, according to the official figures, a lot younger than he was ten years ago. Being younger than you were ten years ago is even more impressive than being only two years *older* than you were ten years ago. But relax, because the average human being doesn't exist either.

I think I would rather exist and be ten years older than I was in 1970, than not exist and be only two years older or a whole lot younger. Wouldn't you?

Inflation: Cause and Cure

"You are old, Father William," the young man said
  "And your hair has become very white;
And yet you incessantly stand on your head—
  Do you think, at your age, it is right?"

Charles Lutwidge Dodgson, known to the world the last
hundred years or so as Lewis Carroll, had a pretty good eye for
people standing on their heads. And he might have noticed that
the wonderful world of economics has an upside-down, inside-
out quality about it these days, not at all unlike the world Alice
found behind the looking glass. Recently, as we have been taking steps to break the back of inflation, that world has become
"curiouser and curiouser."

For example, just as there were many things Alice found
hard to understand in Wonderland, so it is with many of us as
we enter the world of money matters. " . . . They drew all manner of things, everything that begins with an M . . . such as
mouse-traps, and the moon, and memory, and muchness—you
know you say things are 'much of a muchness. . . .'"

Here is the world of the money supply,
Where the monster Inflation must live and must die.
With interest rates rising incredibly tall,
So that no one can get any money at all.

We will slay the fierce dragon right here in his den,
And then everything will be peachy again.
But first there are dangers we all have to face,
Where depression is lurking all over the place.

"Beware the Jabberwock, my son!
  The jaws that bite, the claws that catch!
Beware the Jubjub bird, and shun
  The frumious Bandersnatch!"

For properly, if understood,
Rising interest rates are good.

And if businesses are forced to close,
It's not, as commonly supposed,
A bad thing—not so bad at all.
Someday those interest rates will fall.

And if a lot of jobs are lost,
If that's the price it has to cost
To slay the double-digit beast,
We shouldn't mind it in the least.

Tut-tut, my child, it's not so hard
To do without one's credit card.
Do not complain and do not grouse
Because you can't afford a house.

Economists are quite aloof
To needs for floor and walls and roof.
They have a very different feeling
When they say floor, when they say ceiling.

The answer now is sure and swift.
Now mortgage interest rates will shift.
They'll fluctuate, as you will see,
And be whatever they will be.

Inflation will not go away.
It just seems to get worse.
Inflation can be understood
Inside this little verse:

" 'If seven maids with seven mops
    Swept it for half a year,
Do you suppose,' the Walrus said,
    'That they could get it clear?'
'I doubt it,' said the Carpenter,
    And shed a bitter tear."

We've got to break inflation's back
The Fed, it's said, has spoken.
And that's just swell, but can you tell
Whose back is being broken?

Pg 173-4
is missing

8kl.54
O

Osgood, Charles
    There's nothing that
I wouldn't do if you
would be my POSSLQ

5/82